STOICISM

How to Apply Stoicism in Everyday Life

(Complete Beginner's Guide to the Stoic Way of Life)

Anne Thomas

Published by Tomas Edwards

Stoicism: How to Apply Stoicism in Everyday Life (Complete Beginner's Guide to the Stoic Way of Life)

ISBN 978-1-989744-75-8

Legal & Disclaimer

The information contained in this book is not designed to replace or take the place of any form of medicine or professional medical advice. The information in this book has been provided for educational and entertainment purposes only.

The information contained in this book has been compiled from sources deemed reliable, and it is accurate to the best of the Author's knowledge; however, the Author cannot guarantee its accuracy and validity and cannot be held liable for any errors or omissions. Changes are periodically made to this book. You must consult your doctor or get professional medical advice before using any of the suggested remedies, techniques, or information in this book.

Upon using the information contained in this book, you agree to hold harmless the Author from and against any damages, costs, and expenses, including any legal fees potentially resulting from the application of any of the information provided by this guide. This disclaimer applies to any damages or injury caused by the use and application, whether directly or indirectly, of any advice or information presented, whether for breach of contract, tort, negligence, personal injury, criminal intent, or under any other cause of action.

You agree to accept all risks of using the information presented inside this book. You need to consult a professional medical practitioner in order to ensure you are both able and healthy enough to participate in this program.

Table of Contents

Introduction

Stoicism is a school of thought, which thrived in roman and Greek antiquity. It had been among the loftiest and an exalted philosophy in the history of western civilizations.

Stoics have always thought that the goal of all inquiry is to provide a mode of conduct characterized by the tranquility of mind and certainty of moral worth.

For the first philosopher, as for all posts of the schools, its pursuit and knowledge are held to be ends in themselves. The age was a period of transition, along with the stoic philosopher was its representative. The culture was in the making. The legacy with Athens as its pioneer; was to undergo modifications, although continuous. If, as with Socrates, to know is to know oneself, rationality as the sole means by which something outside of the self might be achieved may be said to be the hallmark of stoic belief.

Stoicism introduced an arc vitae for folks to whom the state arranged cosmos and looked like the mirror of a uniform, serene. The reason could show the source of worth that is unyielding, and the constancy of order motive became the model for human presence. Virtue is an intrinsic quality of the earth, no less inexorable in relation to people than are the laws of nature.

The Stoics believe that perceptions the cornerstone of understanding that is true. In logic, their comprehensive presentation of this subject comes from understanding, yielding not only the conclusion that understanding is potential but also that certainty is possible, on the analogy of the incorrigibility of perceptual expertise. To these, the planet is made up of material items, together with some few exceptions (e.g., significance), and also, the irreducible component in all things is an appropriate reason, which communicates the entire world as celestial fire. This motive or destiny, in, governs matters, such as bodies. The world, in its own entirety, is ruled as to display the grandeur of the structure, which may function from the law as a benchmark for humanity and the ordering of lifestyle.

Therefore, humans' objective would be to live in accordance with nature. Stoic theory is based as one town; on the view, the entire world is a motto. People, as world citizens, have a responsibility and devotion. They need to play an active part in world events, recalling that appropriate and virtue actions are exemplified by the world.

Thus, obligation moral value and justice are stoic emphases, together with a sternness of thoughts. For the ethical individual, neither is merciful nor reveals shame because each indicates a deviation from responsibility and by the fated requirement that rules the entire world.

Nonetheless, using its loftiness of soul and its focus on the person's essential worth the topics of international brotherhood and the benevolence of celestial character make stoicism among the most attractive characteristics.

Close to the end of the 4th-century BCE called Zeno of Citium (modernday Cyprus) dropped his freight, and hardly escaped with his life, even at a shipwreck not far from Athens. Having made it to the town, he walked right into a bookshop in which the proprietor was declaiming xenophon's memorabilia, a publication about Socrates. Struck from the words at which he might find himself a philosopher impressed with the idea of people like Socrates, Zeno requested the bookseller. "There's just one walking down the road at this time," answered the bookseller, pointing into crates of the best, among the most well-known philosophers in Athens at the moment. Crates were followed by Zeno and became his pupil while beginning his own college. The Zidonians, since they were understood, spoke philosophy in people and met, under a colonnade from the agora stained, or referred to as the stoa poikile porch. They were referred to since the Zidonians one tongue did not roll-off.

Why am I telling this story?

What could philosophy create 24 centuries past maybe teach us, worldly individuals of the 21st century, together with our mobiles, social networking, and bogus news? Quite a bit, as it turns out.

That's why stoicism continues to be around the resurgence of late, with major media outlets covering the story of why so many have begun reading Seneca, Epictetus, and Marcus Aurelius. In a feeling, no one should be surprised by this. Stoicism is by now, not the sole, and definitely not the historical doctrine that attracts individuals. When there are not many card-carrying epicureans or even cynics today, there are approximately 500 million Buddhists and nearly 2. 5 billion

Muslims. In addition, though Christianity is faith and Buddhism is a religion and a philosophy, we need to remember that all religions may also be philosophies of existence because all of them come together with both basic elements of standard philosophies: a metaphysics, i.e., an account of the way the planet hangs together, along with also integrity, i.e., an account of the way we ought to act on earth.

Thus, one approach to answering this question, "why stoicism?" Is to point out that the exact same could be requested for lots of different philosophies and religions, the response being in part exactly the same: since human beings have not changed much in the intervening millennia. Sure, we've advanced technologies, but we want the very same items (shelter, food, safety, esteem, love, a sense of significance), and therefore are fearful of the very same items (poverty, shame, illness, death). Our ancestors figured out the fundamental answers to our needs and anxieties in the time period moving out of several centuries prior to the modern age to the beginning of this. In addition, that is now the reason why we read these.

Chapter 1: What Exactly Is Stoicism?

Stoicism means indifference to all emotions, whether it be pain, pleasure, hate or the love of impassiveness. However, the philosophy of

Stoicism is completely different and encompasses a very different set of ideas.

Stoicism, in short, is a series of mental techniques and ways of life that allow you to decrease and virtually eliminate all negative emotions such as anger, fear, anxiety, and dissatisfaction, while simultaneously building up a tide of pure joy inside yourself.

One of the fundamental beliefs associated with Stoicism is that there is a common law, one that is unchanging for all men and women regardless of their acceptance of Stoicism. To study or to believe in Stoicism is to simply come to terms with and accept the already existing fact of this common law and governing reason; to then use this knowledge to control and conquer one's self would be the incorporation of its practice. However, it is unrealistic to believe in the assimilation of a singular principle into an entire empire to believe that every citizen will follow a single set of moral principles and way of life. So, being unrealistic is not enough of an excuse to forgo necessity, therefore we continue on to a deeper point. The philosophy of Stoicism, the idea of using reason to understand the common law of nature in order to conquer the passions and judge correctly and unbiased, even so far as to cast judgment upon one's self, is strikingly and inherently flawed in its own practice. When one uses such an unpassionate rule of the mind, one must look not only inward, but also at the very principle of Stoicism itself. Ironically, the flaw in Stoicism may be seen only from the view of a Stoic, from the vantage point of one already under Stoic influence; one must use Stoicism to accurately analyze its principles.

The basic teachings of Stoicism is that bad emotions come from bad judgement and the core of Stoicism is to overcome these destructive emotions through control. They also say that true happiness is achieved through virtue.

Stoics presented the philosophy as a way of life through which you can become sage. A sage is someone who has achieved ethical and intellectual perfection.

Many philosophers (including Seneca) emphasized the belief that happiness is achieved through virtue. With this being true, then a sage would be immune to misfortune, since misfortune causes unhappiness and through virtue there is no unhappiness.

It's not difficult to envision a lot of profound Greek thinkers, philosophers, astrologers, etc. who identified with a false sense of superiority based on some profound understandings they had. It's also not farfetched to envision many Roman politicians, military strategists, gladiators and such who saw Stoicism as a manner of behavior that kept them elevated from the uniformed masses. No wonder Stoicism is rampant in today's society, especially when thousands of years have passed in which joy and sorrow suppressed rather than welcomed through the various indicators of feelings and emotions that mask truths. A wise man once said, "Truth is sorrow". This is why society doesn't support the investigations of life failings and resultant wounds, nor is there a wide-spread understanding relative to how this attitude is interpreted in the intangible and manifested on the tangible level. Without sorrow, there is no recognition of joy; a natural frequency or sine wave of life that traverses the entire spectrum of the human consciousness. Society seems to have difficulty discerning outward appearances with a degree of accuracy; stories that would have you believe in courage, strength, and wisdom of a person who has gone from a down-trodden placement to that of a winner, from hardship to prosperity, or from victimization to victorious are based often on beliefs associated with a stoic attitude, not applicable truths.

Stoicism doesn't allow others to sense what it means to falter and fall; to pick yourself up and get on with living in such a way that doesn't keep others in the dark; questioning their own interpretations, which may be appropriate, but lacking a certain degree of maturity. Courage, sincerity, and authenticity reside in the willingness to humbly acknowledge infinite unknown factors that were part of an equation that was faulty from the start. Unbridled joy and ease does not mask the intangible wounds of our psyche, it puts life in perspective to the essence of our wisdom which is not achieved through Stoicism. Stoicism also concerns itself heavily with fate and human free will. They believe in determinism (the idea that all future events are controlled by all past events in a philosophy similar to fate) but they also believe in individual free will. This mix of belief produces both a sense of acceptance of what will be will be, while still trying to change the future for the better. Stoicism also puts a lot of importance into the idea of logic. The belief is that only through logic and truth can knowledge be attained. Although this seems like common logic in today's society, it is important to look back when the temples told you why a storm had blown in and why the stars had the patterns they had. One of the greatest lines of Stoicism is as follows. Quoted from Marcus Aurelius. "Say to yourself in the early morning: I shall meet today ungrateful, violent, treacherous, envious, uncharitable men. All of these things have come upon them, through ignorance of real good and ill... I can neither be harmed by any of them, for no man will involve me in wrong, nor can I be angry with my kinsman or hate him; for we have come into the world to work together".

Chapter 2: How To Deal With Yourself When Life Gets Tough

Let's face it. Sometimes life is not easy. There are days when you can't catch a break. Sometimes, these days cannot be prevented because you will be hit with something that is beyond your control. You are let go from your job. Your significant other breaks up with you. You have an argument with a close friend. You have a fender-bender while driving home. Whatever the circumstance is, it has jostled your emotions. If you sink into this, you are at risk of doing something you will regret later. This is why it is so important not to let yourself get worked up to the point where you can no longer control your emotions.

The first thing you need to do is stop for a moment. Whatever you are doing, drop it just for a little while. If you are talking to someone else, and this is the source of your distress, you definitely need to stop the conversation for a little while. You might think you need to have the argument out now, but you are upset and so are they. The only thing that will happen is that the two of you will become more upset with each other. Just step away from the situation. Do something that calms you down. Go for a run. Listen to music. Write in your journal. Call a friend or family member who you can trust to keep your secrets and vent to them. Let your initial impulses come and go until you can think rationally about the situation.

A common practice among stoics is to brace themselves for the worst-case scenario. The goal in this is not to be pessimistic. It is to be prepared. When you have accepted the worst things that can happen, you will be able to deal with them and operate under those circumstances. I'm going to drag a theatre motto into this—"The show must go on". When you're putting on a performance, things are going to go wrong. No matter how many times you rehearsed, no matter how much the crew has poured over the lights and setting, there are going to be mistakes made. Even Broadway performances that have turned into well-oiled machines suffer these kinds of mishaps. Someone will forget a line. A prop will be dropped. A setting transition will be a little too early or late. Miscommunications will happen among the sound technicians. However, there is no time to stop and lament about the mistake. This will only cause more mistakes to happen and then it will be apparent to the audience that this play was not well-prepared. Instead, the cast and crew are to improvise in these circumstances.

A stoic does not sink into stress. This is a difficult thing to avoid, especially if you are a person who is more prone to the sensation of anxiety. It might feel like you will not be able to overcome this feeling. When you are feeling overcome by stress, ground yourself. Part of accepting your current circumstances is to not burden yourself with more than what is really happening. This means don't worry about things that haven't happened yet. If your boss hasn't called your performance into question, do not worry about them firing you. If all seems to be going well in your romantic relationship and they haven't said anything that would hint at breaking up with you, trust that it is secure. To make a long story short, don't borrow trouble and create problems for yourself. This takes time away from doing something about the ones you actually have.

A psychological technique that is often used when someone is becoming too emotional is known as mindful grounding. This means you ground yourself into the present whenever you are worried about the past or future. If your focus is on either of those timelines, you are not being mindful, and you are wasting time. To alleviate this, you pull yourself back into the present by focusing on what is happening in the real world. This is done by turning your attention to whatever is around you. Use your senses. If you see a painting in the room, focus on its different colors and patterns. If there is something playing on the television or radio, listen in. Reach out for an object in your vicinities, such as a pencil, decoration, or even your shirt sleeve, and touch it.

There is also something to faking it until you make it. If you let yourself become consumed by distressing feelings, they are only going to become stronger. If you are going through a time where you are feeling down, you are not going to want to dedicate yourself to self-care, but this is the time where it is the most important. Sometimes you will need to just get up and do something even though you are not feeling the motivation to do it. Spending your time alone in your room, not seeing anyone or putting any effort into your appearance or physical health, is going to make your life feel bleaker as this goes on longer. If you are feeling down about yourself, take a shower or bath. Get dressed, put on makeup if you choose to do so, and generally do the things that make you feel like you look good. You've probably heard the idea that if you look good, you will feel good, and there is truth to it. If you go out somewhere after rolling out of bed and not putting effort into your appearance, you will subconsciously act more timid. Even if someone is interested in talking to you, you will likely avoid them because you are convinced they are starting at a flaw of yours. You will want to just run your errands and get back home, hoping no one notices you. However, when you have dressed up, you will go out putting your best foot forward. You will be comfortable talking to people. In fact, you will probably be bolder than usual. You will show people more of your true personality and therefore establish a stronger connection. You are also living with arete when you do this. You have put time and effort into creating something. In this case, it is your look, which is important in today's world. When you go to an interview for a job, the way you look and present yourself will matter, and advancing in your career is essential to living with virtue.

Next, we're going to talk about stress management. Stress is a common problem for people right now. The fact is that that we are juggling more things than we have in the past. For example, work and school have been changed by the internet. While you have access to more information, it also makes for more things you need to keep track of. Many people have multiple work phones, and this means they have to keep up with all of their notifications, and in addition, they have to keep an eye out for emails, social media messages, and more. On top of that, there are family responsibilities and anything else a person is involved in. Many people are finding it difficult to stay on top of things and spend a great deal of time wondering how they are going to finish all of their tasks for the day.

All of this points to the fact that you must have a means of stress relief, or you are not going to be able to keep it in check, and therefore your emotions will spiral out of control.

You need to set a time that you are going to think about the things that are bothering you. Once that time is up, you have got to hold yourself to putting all of your worries away. When you continue to feed your anxiety about something, not only are you not actually doing anything about the problem, but you are putting both your physical and mental health at risk. Stress that is prolonged increases in intensity. If it is not alleviated, it can cause you to have a nervous breakdown. You definitely will not make the best judgment calls when you are in this state of mind. It can escalate to panic attacks. When you are experiencing anxiety, your heart rate increases dramatically. Over time this will cause problems with your blood pressure. Some people have even had heart attacks due to stress.

It is easier to manage the problem before it gets to that point than to try to relieve it once you are there. This is why you need to learn to relax and also be able to recognize when you are at your limit and need to take some time to focus solely on your mental health, otherwise known as a mental health day. You've probably heard of these before, and they are actually quite helpful. If you are feeling burned out, putting more pressure on yourself isn't going to do you any favors. Think about how, when your phone's battery runs out, there is nothing more it will be able to do until you put it on the charger. Humans need to recharge. There's only so long that you can "run on fumes" and keep going. It is a lesson in self-preservation and survivability to learn when you have reached your limit.

There are some subtle signs to watch out for before it gets to the point where you're in danger of a breakdown. For one, you're more irritable than usual. Your interactions with people have gotten more confrontational, and you are quick to take things others say as an insult. Stress also causes people to cry more easily. Emotional distress can also manifest through physical symptoms. In particular, you will feel fatigued and taking a nap doesn't help. Stress is tiring on the body because it causes many of its organs to over-function. When you read through these symptoms and relate to them, you are in desperate need of a mental health day.

Make a plan to do it this weekend. The first thing you need to do is unplug. Make yourself unavailable by phone and other media. This way, you have no risk of any drama starting with anyone. After that, there really is no right or wrong way to go about this day. It will start to become intuitive. Your mind and body will tell you what you need. Only think about helping your present self.

One of the most painful and unhelpful things to do for your psyche is to wish for things to be different that have already happened. This is going to be a difficult habit to let go of because we are creatures who want what we want. It begins early in life. As children, we get upset about not having won some contest. As we get older, we have to deal with bigger disappointments, such as someone we have a crush on choosing someone else and another person being picked for a job we wanted. It is easy to feel defeated about these types of disappointments and like they would not have happened if there wasn't something wrong with you. However, this is a form of personalizing something that should be taken with a grain of salt. Sometimes someone will not return the feelings you have for them. If you are turned down for a job, they just have a different personality or skill set in mind. It is not out of personal feelings against you. Sometimes you will want to be a part of a group of friends, and it doesn't work out. It might not even be that they dislike you. You could just not click with them. You are two different people, and so you are not a good fit for them. Someone not wanting to be friends with you does not mean you are unlikable.

It just means you are looking in the wrong places for friends. Try finding people whose interests are more aligned with yours.

We've talked about needing to take responsibility for your actions. No matter how good we try to be, there will still be times where we do something wrong. You will never go through life without doing things that wrong people, and often we cause the most pain when we are trying to not to upset anyone. You are going to hurt someone's feelings at some point, and when you do this, you need to learn to apologize. This is one of the hardest things for anyone to do. We want to think of ourselves as good people, and when we have to admit we have done something hurtful to someone else, that goes against this belief. There is also the natural human instinct to self-protect. It does not make you a bad person. Everyone wants to be the good guy in disagreements. However, you will have to move past this if you want to preserve relationships and live with integrity.

When we do something wrong, we need to apologize to the person whose feelings we have damaged. There is a right and wrong way to apologize, and it is not about the exact verbiage. It is about the spirit in which you give it.

For one, do not give a non-apology. When you are trying to express regret for hurting someone is not the time to voice a grievance you have about them or defend yourself. What I mean when I say a non-apology is one where the ultimate goal is to defend oneself. This could mean shuffling the blame onto the other person, for example, acknowledging you did something wrong but then going on to say it was provoked by them. The best way to avoid doing this is by never, under any circumstances, letting yourself say the words "I'm sorry, but". There is a saying that claims that every word before the word "but" it canceled out by that word. It might come off to the other person like you were only saying that as required etiquette but do not really feel it.

It is best to make the apology short and succinct. Even though your first impulse might be to try to make a speech, if you do this, you will come off as rambling. It might also seem like you are trying to put the focus on you. Just state what you are sorry for. It means more than you might think to a person when you explicitly say what you have done. It not only lets it be known that you know what you did that was wrong, but it also shows that you are willing to own up to it. It makes the apology feel more sincere than if you talk vaguely about it. It will also give you a sense of feeling like the bandage has been ripped off. You will be able to move on from this incident.

Admit it was wrong to do. Say something that has the effect of "I know I behaved badly there. However, you word it, you are admitting that was not your finest moment, and this will be validating for them. One of the most difficult things for people to deal with is feeling like they did not get closure or that someone who has done something wrong to them does not feel remorse about it. They will not even be as upset about the act itself as they will about the lack of remorse. Your character will be improved in their eyes when you take responsibility for whatever it is that you have done

While you need to admit when you have done wrong, there is a caveat. Make this point briefly and then move on. Do not grovel about this fact or say something like, "I'm such a horrible friend." You might think it is expressing deep regret or that saying bad things about yourself if a part of taking responsibility, but if you do too much flagellating yourself, it will seem like a manipulative tactic. When someone is doing this, it sets off an instinct in others to ease their pain. This means they will need to be giving comfort to someone else while they are the ones whose feelings need to be tended to.

Stoicism means knowing how to deal when things do not go your way, knowing that the longer you spend lamenting about the disappointment, the longer you will put off doing something to improve your situation. Mourning for what you have lost must come to an end. What has been lost is now in the past, and you need to think about what you have in the present. We talked earlier about sending a job application and having it denied. This is understandably upsetting, but you must pull yourself together and send out another application. That is the only way you are going to be hired by anyone. You can be angry about what happened, insist that the company made a mistake and be kicked down by this, but by the end of all of that you will still need a job. You have to find a way to become hopeful again as you continue your job hunt. When you send your resume to another company, think of this as another opportunity. The possibility of being hired has come about again. The more you send out, the more you increase your chances of being called back. This is how you can pull yourself out of an unpleasant situation and create your own outcomes.

Another thing that will help you is to ask someone who has been in the workforce for a long time to look at your resume and give you advice on how to make it better. This might feel a little daunting and even embarrassing because when you do this, they will have suggestions and constructive criticisms to give you. This means you will need to humble yourself enough to open yourself up to this. This does not mean that you are admitting to being bad at writing a resume; it means you are invested enough in it that you will call in someone with more experience to guide you. You cannot afford to be prideful in this situation. No one comes out of the gate knowing everything, and candidates who were proceeded with instead of you are not inherently better than you. For all you know, this was the hundredth application they had sent and every other time before that they had been rejected. They'd had to craft and revise the way they presented themselves to potential employers. The first time you go to an interview will not be your best performance. For one, it will be a new experience so you will be nervous. You will not have your plan of how to portray yourself fully rounded out. In fact, for most people, their first try is a debacle. If this is the way it happens for you, do not become discouraged or feel ashamed of yourself. Just figure out what you can do better next time and congratulate yourself for having that first experience being interviewed. Each time this happens, you will learn something new. Eventually, you will no longer be nervous about it because you will have become used to this process. You will also have a better idea of what to do. You will speak more confidently and learn how to give quick and thoughtful answers to questions that you cannot predict.

If you are sending in applications each and every day, going to interviews, and putting all of your effort into it, you are going to get results. The idea that there are people the world favors and ones that nothing ever works out for is false. This is self-defeating thought that causes people to take their hands off the reins in their own life.

Another common misconception about life is that strength is about who can do the most vicious things. A person who has an unpleasant disposition and is easily annoyed will always say that life is difficult and that you need to be the one who strikes first before they get you. What they do not realize is that they create a lot of their own problems with their confrontational attitude. They make their own life difficult because they turn every interaction they have with another person into a fight. Because they do this, they are constantly having to fight, not realizing they would not have to do this if they did not approach others in a confrontational manner. This is also not the way to handle it when someone does want to start a conflict with you. In fact, that is what we will talk about in our final chapter.

Chapter 3: A Brief History Of Stoicism

Ancient Stoicism

"An unexamined life is not worth living."

Stoicism develops from ancient Greek ideas that first gathered most prominently around Socrates and then Plato's Academy. Zeno, a merchant from Citium (modern-day Cyprus), is generally regarded as the founder of the Stoic school of philosophy in the early 3rd century BCE in Athens.

It's said that Zeno ended up in Athens because of a shipwreck. He was a prosperous merchant with a shipload of merchandise he intended to sell there, but apparently, the weather wasn't cooperative. Or maybe the captain had a little too much to drink. Regardless, the ship went down, and he lost everything. He barely escaped drowning. As the story goes, Zeno made his way, broke and probably a big mess, kind of like a homeless guy these days, to the agora of Athens, which was a sort of ongoing giant farmers market in Athens, the bustling center of life. It's said that Zeno observed later in life, "When I lost all my wealth coming to Athens, I, in fact, became a wealthy man."

Rather than a lamb skewer, though, it's said Zeno used his last few coins to buy a copy of the great sayings of Socrates. Perusing it, he then asked the bookseller, "Where is there a man like this?" The bookseller replied, "Well, Socrates is dead, long time ago. Poison or something. But ask him over there," He was pointing to a guy who looked like he was homeless, too. It was Crates, who was a practitioner of Cynicism, a philosophy which had broken off from The Academy, the school Plato had started.

Zeno started up a conversation with Crates, the Cynic. As the story goes, Zeno followed him for a while. But after a few years, Zeno became disillusioned with Cynic philosophy. It was, well, pretty cynical. Cynics thought everybody should go back to nature and live like dogs (kynes), quite literally, which is where the word Cynic comes from. It doesn't sound very appealing to me, either.

Zeno, in time, developed his own philosophy and would lecture on it from painted stoa (porches), from which Stoicism derives its name. Like Cynicism, it was rooted in the idea that philosophy should have practical applications for life as it's lived, mostly that one needs to live in accord with nature. But living like a dog in the street was taking it a little too far. But Zeno's new approach to an active philosophy was evidently well-received, and over time he garnered many followers, some wealthy, some not. He became popular among a few kings, too. He became successful, and his ideas traveled well beyond his lifetime, and were further developed among many ancient Greeks and then Romans.

It was through a man called Epictetus, a Greek slave in fact, and over a hundred years later, that we have the first direct written accounts of Stoicism. And even that was through one of Epictetus' pupils, Arrian. He apparently took excellent notes in class.

Like all schools of philosophy, Stoicism attempted to provide a coherent theory of the universe and of man's place within it. Based on these observations, Stoicism also presents a prescription for the manner in which an individual might live the best possible life. Ancient Stoicism put great store into an ethical plan for one's life, based upon a reasoned appreciation of the nature of the world as well as a frank assessment of an individual's place within it. It posits that man is intrinsically a social creature. But that also each individual is an island unto themselves.

A "general goo" and the peace of mind of an individual were inter-related. An individual should, indeed, strive to live a life of virtue in line with nature. The Stoic philosophy and its prescriptions for daily living caught on and became a widely popular school of philosophy as well as the manner of conduct.

Unlike much of Greek philosophy until around that time, Stoicism addressed the issues of daily life. How do I conduct myself with others? Upon what foundation of understanding should I act? And to what end? It's been suggested that to some degree, the emergence of Stoicism comes along with the emergence of modern consciousness. Who am I? What is my place in the universe? And, most importantly, if I'm going just to die someday, then why should I even care?

Stoicism addresses such questions by proposing a simple, clearly stated well. Human happiness (or well-being might be a closer translation of the Greek), derived from living in harmony with the flowing of life, a life whose very nature is change and constant flux. This is only possible with a sober application of reason, which, in turn, requires mastery over the unruly disturbances brought about by our emotional, instinct-based, reactions to the world around us. Emotions are often disruptive and turn us away from our reasoning capacities, our clear understanding of our true place in the universe, which is to play our role with virtue and in harmony with the world around us.

Such an understanding, they reasoned, should lead us to live moderately. Not to deny the needs or impulses of the body, but to give them their proper weight and to understand that indulgence beyond what is necessary cannot lead to happiness. It clouds the judgment and threatens to remove our actions from any possible wise and discernably good effect. The goal is not necessarily to deny feeling but to bring it into happy accord with our mind, the dominant faculty of reason, and so with all those others who live in the world around us.

Stoicism has perhaps been too closely associated with ideas of self-deprivation and self-flagellation, particularly in a Christian worldview, which came much later, with its notions of original sin. Such assumptions miss the point entirely. In fact, Stoicism was and is a philosophy that is concerned with the prescriptions for wresting the most satisfaction and deepest enjoyment from life. A sense of meaning and purpose in one's action, and of one's place in the world, any serious practicing Stoic could tell you, is the point of and product of a Stoic life.

Modern Stoicism

"Man can detach from immediate environments and choose

an attitude regarding himself, thus attaining inner freedom

and a basis for meaningful action."

- Victor Frankl

Stoicism and its precepts are enjoying a broad resurgence recently. Based upon renewed scholarly interest in Stoicism among 20th-century scholars, the basic Stoic ideas have been found to be quite applicable to the conundrums of 21st-century life. Some of the new Stoics are also actual scholars, people who study the received texts from various points of academic inquiry. Other modern Stoics are folks who've simply seen the logic and wisdom in the Stoic concepts, and how they benefit them in their lives. Indeed, there is a wide array of groups on social media that now share Stoic precepts and views on the Stoic lifestyle. There are numerous books about the practical application of Stoicism in daily life. There's even a "Stoicon" convention that now meets every year in differing locales all over the world with tens of thousands of attendees.

Earlier in the 20th century, and still today, Stoic concepts have been adapted to therapeutic theories broadly informing all manner of schools of therapy, thanks to such influential 20th century psychologists as Dr. Albert Ellis, Aaron T. Beck and, perhaps most notably, Viktor Frankl, who survived imprisonment in a Nazi concentration camp thanks to concepts and practices derived directly from the ancient Stoics. This is perhaps the most extreme example of the usefulness of Stoicism, and one which hopefully no one will have to experience again.

The core principle of Stoicism might be stated as follows: It's not what happens that troubles us, but our response to what happens. And over our response to events, we do in fact have control." Of course, this is easier said than done.

One key problem regarding Stoicism as a viable philosophy in the 20th century has to do with our understanding of nature, of the great changes in our perceptions of the nature of the world over the last two thousand years. We are a tiny species trapped upon a little rock in an ever-expanding universe, a universe that doesn't seem too much care whether we prosper or not. Science has also brought about technological changes that have resulted, among much good, in human inflicted suffering on mass industrial scales unimaginable in Zeno's time. Can such a philosophy work, based as it was upon archaic ideas of nature as a "good" in and of itself? Wasn't it then "nature" that developed nuclear weapons and Nazi concentration camps?

Aside from merely semantic arguments, it has been proposed that Stoicism's insistence than one life in accord with such a "Nature" can be usefully transposed into an insistence that one lives in accord with simply what is, with "the facts" of the world. Upon this foundation, Stoic precepts are still useful. Some would even suggest that Stoic precepts are even more pertinent now. They would suggest that acceptance of the world around one as it is, as our technologies allow for ever greater alienating consequences, is all that more important. Regardless, both then and now, as a practical application of a philosophy, the question is unchanged and might best be expressed like this: How do I live the best life within an everchanging flowing world as I can best understand it?

Needless to say, within the sweep of ancient Stoicism, which is 500 years give or take, and within modern Stoic practice today, there's considerable divergence. But it wouldn't be appropriate for our purposes to spend any more effort in detailing it. As you progress, though, you may very well want to investigate all these various threads and differing views.

For now, let's begin by observing that Stoics everywhere are deeply involved with the questions regarding individual agency. What exactly do I control? And what do I not?

Chapter 4: What Is Stoicism?

How often are you troubled with your own thoughts? That continuous tommyrot of crud running in your mind? These unnecessary thoughts of worry and negativity could be the reason for your grief or sorrow. Here's the good news: you can take control over your thinking via the amazing and practically methodical philosophy of stoicism.

Stoicism is the popular antique Greek philosophy founded by Zeno of Citium in Athens while it was precariously in the third century BC. To be stoic is to be in the eye of a hurricane—to remain still and calm in the middle of whirlwinds of chaos and destruction. It's just not a philosophy, but a way of living which transforms the lives of many.

There are some morals of stoicism, such as prudence, fortitude, justice, and moderation.

It has been practiced by many great people, one of whom was the Roman king Marcus Aurelius. The emperor was a paradoxical example of stoicism. Another famous historical person was Epictetus, and beyond him there are many more examples.

What Does Stoicism do to Mankind?

Stoicism gives us power over our thought process and allows us to become resilient enough to face the hardships of life. It can also save a soul from chaos. It is simply about endurance (mental, not necessarily physical) and our capability for patience as well as controlling negative emotions. There are many other things that happen to a stoic person such as a renewed admiration for reality, higher sense of justice, believing in themselves, and a better attitude towards life in general. Simply put, stoicism enlightens the mind and promotes better living through adopting self-control over devastating thoughts. It is the art of balancing human thoughts and emotions.

You can master your thoughts and improve your energy. Doesn't it seem fantastically empowering to get to know yourself better, control your thoughts in a way that benefits you, and find harmony in life? Stoicism embraces acceptance, and whether the outcome of any situation is good or bad it keeps you calm. It teaches you to accept reality.

According to science, the human mind is full of memories. But where does this memory come from? I'd say experience rather than thoughts. There can be certain experiences which create specific thoughts. For instance, a trauma during childhood may never be forgotten. This trauma can give your thoughts an everlasting impression. Thoughts are the fundamentals of human nature. You are what you think. Perception makes a huge difference.

According to the great Marcus Aurelius, "Very little is needed to make a happy life, it is all within yourself, in your way of thinking" (Marcus Aurelius, Hard, Marcus Aurelius & Fronto, 2011).

Let's understand this deeply. Thoughts are seeds which grow inside us. When you can grow a rose (good thought), then why should you grow weed (bad thought)? Every single day and every second of your life you are performing some kind of action. These could be physical, they could be mental, or emotional. In their entirety, these actions are very closely related to feelings, or you could say emotions. These thoughts make feelings, and feelings make emotions. Emotions in turn produce chemicals in our body and mind. In an easy language, you can call them "hormones."

Thoughts, feelings, emotions, and hormones give birth to some sort of energy within the body. It could be positive energy or negative energy. Stoicism shuts down negative thoughts and negative behaviors. It promotes a positive attitude towards life. It lets you see reality for what it really is and helps you with acceptance, too. Ultimately, stoicism changes one's mindset.

Epictetus was a Stoic philosopher of the 1st century AD, and together with Marcus Aurelius and Seneca he's known for being one of the big figures in Stoic philosophy. If you read more about him, you will find out that his teachings are actually quite enthralling.

Epictetus spent a portion of his life as a slave in the city of Hierapolis in Asia Minor. The fact that Epictetus was once a slave gives real credence and authority to his teachings. As you may know, stoicism is essentially about living as contentedly with life as you possibly can, no matter what the circumstances are. I can't help but feel that Epictetus' experience as a slave would have taught him a lot about acceptance and contentment. That really does shine through in his words.

He has penned down some of the best quotes and specific ideas for stoic teachers which I think are both relevant to us and also representative of stoicism as a whole. He said that everyone has to die, and he must have to as well. He explained his slavery by saying that his body was chained, but not his mind. Further, he added that no one could take his smile from him. I think these ideas are a good introduction into the central stoic concept: the idea that we are ultimately in control of our impressions and feelings. According to the Stoics, our will is our most precious possession as human beings.

Our will is our ability to make reasonable and sound judgments about our circumstances, and although our bodies might suffer or be imprisoned, our will never has to submit. Therefore, we can remain content even in the direst of circumstances. The only manacles that could ever truly entrap our minds are our own thoughts. Likewise, our mind has the power to undo all manacles which might be thrust upon us. We should all be familiar with the idea of acquiring contentment through the use of our will.

It's also worth considering the way that the Stoics view the world. The world can be divided into two broad categories, and this is a really easy equation. There are things which are out of our control—that is, all externalities and all circumstances outside of ourselves—and then there are things which are in our control and can all be reduced down to our will. The will is critically important, as we can use it to stop those externalities from disrupting our internal sense of contentment or equanimity. There are many quotes of Marcus' where he refers to luck and will. His words are so powerfully depicted that he used fortune in place of circumstances and faculty instead of will. Thus it's clear that our situations create our fortunes and our will can teach us a lesson or two.

The question is, why should we let circumstances override our will? The answer is to be happy. Now back to the word equanimity. It's a word often associated with stoicism and it typically is taken to mean composure, impartiality, or impassiveness. But there are more sources than just stony-faced acceptance. Stoicism is also brimming with a whole lot of gratitude. Gratitude for the fact that we are inhabiting this universe or at the scale a grandeur of this universe. So it's not right to dismiss this philosophy as being simply about tolerating bad things. Stoicism is a pair theistic philosophy, meaning that all things are viewed as being parts in a sacred whole. There's another quote which nicely illustrates that idea. That quote says every human is connected to another. Man is also united with God, which is the supreme power of all. Basically, it says that we should be proud members of this divinely ordained universe.

But even so, we can't forget that stoicism is very concerned with obligations. It's not enough for us to live lives of perfect pleasure. The condition of us having pleasure necessitates that we are also exposed to all the pain that the universe might throw at us. We need to accept it all as part of the whole. We can't pick or choose what life throws at us. Everything is delivered in one incessant stream of totality. This requires us to have a broader perspective on our circumstances than we might be used to having. Epictetus gives us a great example when he asks us to consider that we have broken our leg and appreciate that this is far better than living without legs.

Because we're a part of this grand amazing universe, we need to accept what happens to us for the good of the whole. To get back to that theme of joy and gratitude, another concept is my favorite lesson at the moment. It reminds me that when I'm alone I don't need to consider it a wretched isolated condition. I don't need to feel that I'm missing out. Instead, I can see it as an opportunity for reflecting on the tranquility. Likewise, when I'm in a crowd, there's no reason to withdraw. Instead, I should take the opportunity to engage with my fellow humans to form connections and to interact. This is just really encouraging stoic advice.

Famous Followers of Stoicism

JK Rowling

The immensely successful best-selling author of the HARRY POTTER franchise is indeed a follower of stoic philosophy. She is a continuous follower of Marcus Aurelius, and he is one of her favorite philosophers. His quotes and meditations helped Rowling a lot in her difficult times. Keep in mind that before JK Rowling was a billionaire and a household name, she was just like anyone else. She went through 38 different rejections while taking care of her family as a single mother. Thus, she went through her fair share of adversities and she definitely used the stoic mindset of turning obstacles into the means to press forward. When many other people would have stopped and given up, she kept going. She's definitely a follower of the philosophy.

Neil Strauss

Author of THE GAME, Neil Strauss listed ON THE SHORTNESS OF LIFE by Seneca as one of his favorite books of all time. The interesting thing about this essay by Seneca is that it deals with the fact that we as humans think that life is short, when in reality our life is not short. We have ample time to do what we want. It's just that we waste a lot of our time on petty issues. We think about our neighbor's opinions, we waste time on things that are not going to be fulfilling, or on things that are not really going to matter in the future. Neil Strauss's story is very interesting, because he was selected as a writer for the New York Times Magazine. After some time, he became a pickup artist. He was kicked out of the magazine later. He got over that and became a best-selling author.

Lupe Fiasco

Grammy award-winning conscious rap artist Lupe Fiasco has been known to be an avid reader of Stoicism principles. In one of his songs "Lightwork," he dropped the following line; "Emperor is his alias, but not Marcus Aurelius." Lupe Fiasco has been known to recommend Marcus Aurelius's meditations. He has adapted many quotes and meditations of Marcus Aurelius in his life. Not only that, he even recommends reading and following stoicism and Marcus Aurelius's teachings to everyone. He's basically recommending that everybody absorb the stoic wisdom that has been laid out by the Emperor himself, Marcus Aurelius, so that we can all communicate on the same level and live better lives.

Nassim Nicholas Taleb

Another famous stoic is Nassim Nicholas Taleb, who is a Lebanese American essayist, a scholar aesthetician, as well as a former trader and risk analysis. He is well known for his best-selling book, ANTI FRAGILE, in which he talks about the antifragility of stoic philosophy, especially Seneca's philosophy. According to him, a stoic is someone who can transform their insecurities or fear into prudence, pain into transformation, mistakes into initiation, and desires or wants into the undertaking. He basically just summarized the practical aspects of stoicism. Stoicism has the power to turn all the negatives in your life into something positive as well as turn every situation into a way for you to grow and become better. Stoicism is based on perception. Everything is about perception. So, we can determine the quality of our life by how we choose to perceive the events that happen. This is how famous philosophers have explained about how our life should be. So, a stoic is someone who sees the negative and chooses to transform it into good or into something that can help them.

Bill Clinton

The most famous person on this list is the former president of the United States, Bill Clinton. He was a big fan of Marcus Aurelius and his meditations. As a matter of fact, he said that he read the book once every year while he was president, which would make sense because Marcus Aurelius meditations were kind of like a personal diary for the emperor in which he wrote down notes on how he could live better, become nobler, and live a virtuous life in accordance with nature. Bill Clinton would have received a lot of value in reading these notes, especially because people don't change. Technology changes, but the human condition hasn't changed. We still face the same adversities in leadership and in life. Bill Clinton said that the thing about Marcus Aurelius is that he was deeply spiritual and he understood that life requires balance. His books also show what not to do as an emperor. He has mentioned what he wouldn't do, and that's really important. So clearly, Bill Clinton was heavily influenced by Marcus Aurelius.

All of these are the personalities who totally believe in living their lives to the fullest and not being stuck in any set role which is a part of it. A second is almost a fraction of our lives, and yet our lives are sufficiently long. As long as we can imagine. We need to make sure that we live our lives to the fullest.

Chapter 5: Stoicism And The Mind

You need to learn how to act on principle and not mood. Stoicism can get rid of mental blocks and help us be the best we can be.

We see people every day who lead very creatives lives. We can see the elements of passion, understanding, grit, and expertise. What we overlook are their inner systems, the principles that govern their behavior and mind. When they fail or have to adapt, how do they respond? What do they say to themselves? What is their philosophy?

Philosophy teaches us the way to live. It helps us be better humans. We can overcome our daily problems with philosophy. Some teachings are just for thought and debate, and others are tools to be used in our practical endeavors.

Stoicism holds the most practical and relevant rules for all sorts of artists, writers, and entrepreneurs. Their attention is always on two specific things:

How to live a happy, fulfilling, and wonderful life?

How to turn yourself into a better person?

The main goal is finding inner peace by realizing we only have a short time to live, being aware of impulses, having self-control, overcome adversity. These are meditative practices that will help us live with nature and not against it. We have to understand obstacles we face and never run away. We must turn them into fuel for our fires.

Here are some principles of stoicism that we should embrace and exercise daily. These will help fuel your creativity, improve your life and state of mind, and simplify your workflow. To have creativity, you must be courageous, adaptive, committed, and vulnerable. This requires a mindset that can reverse negative impulses and distractions while we focus our minds and hearts on the things that are important. Balancing all this can be tough.

If we don't have something to guide us with our lives and work, our distractions and excuses will cause us to fall. We act on moods and not principles.

Know That Emotions Come from Inside

Outside forces don't make us feel anything. The things we tell ourselves are what create our feelings. There isn't anything stressful about a blank page, a to-do list, or a blank canvas. Our thoughts are what are stressing us out.

Many will put the responsibility and blame on external things since that is the easiest thing to do. Conflicts begin on the inside of our minds. If we run from reality, emails, deadlines, we are only undermining our self-discipline and harming ourselves.

When you feel resistance or hit an obstacle, don't look around you. Look inside yourself.

To quote Marcus Aurelius, "Today I escaped anxiety. Or no, I discarded it, because it was within me, in my own perceptions – not outside."

Find Somebody You Admire and Let Them Guide You to Honesty

When you first start out in your chosen profession, you might have a hard time finding someone you admire to look up to. The courses you take in college may not even be what you want to do with your life. Lucky for us, the internet can provide us with wonderful people, stories, and examples for us to follow. You can look at someone you respect and see their value, their ethics, and what you can learn from them.

It doesn't matter what you decide to do in life like animation, writing, drawing portraits, creating apps, or being a painter, there is someone out there you could learn from. You can follow their failures, successes, techniques, works, and story. You can listen to podcasts and even send them emails. You could find success patterns and make them a part of your life.

You must realize that you don't need to just compare their life to yours. If your drawings don't get chosen for the new art exhibit or your book didn't get picked to be published in the first month of your career, this doesn't mean you have failed. What you need to do is find something that you can learn from your hero. How can their principles and teachings help you create, learn, or grow? Everybody, and it doesn't matter how successful they are, has someone they look up to.

Life Will Go on After You Have Failed

You might have spent months, possibly years, on your project and have to sadly watch as someone tears it completely apart with bad criticism and then ignore it. You have spent what feels like a lifetime. You have poured your blood, sweat, and tears into. It's your best work ever. You present it and watch as it gets torn to shreds.

To me, it was the same as going through the pains of childbirth and all the people in the delivery room look at your baby and make the comment of how ugly the baby is. It breaks your heart into a million pieces.

This is what it will feel like when you share your most valuable part, and it ends in failure. How you choose to recover from this failure is setting your mind to it and practice. The lessons you can learn from this experience will help you work better. As the old saying goes: No failure, no growth.

To quote Marcus Aurelius: "Does what's happened keep you from acting with humility, honesty, prudence, sanity, self-control, generosity, justice, and other qualities that lets one's nature fulfill itself? Remember this when something threatens to cause pain: the thing itself was no misfortune at all; to endure it and prevail is great good fortune."

Read for Purpose and Apply What You Learn

Reading books about your chosen profession will supply you with endless potential for developing a deeper connection and more awareness. Doing your craft is what makes you more effective. You can prepare your mind by reading. It will help you stay away from mistakes, but eventually, you must face reality. This reality could be a lesson, success, or failure.

The reason we need to be educated is not just to learn, but to facilitate better decisions and spark creativity. If you can find and read self-help books, it will inspire you to change. Can you follow your principles in the face of an angry person, a rude customer, or a troll?

A quote by Epictetus sums it up: "Don't just say you have read books. Show that through them you have learned to think better, to be a more discriminating and reflective person. Books are the training weights of the mind. They are very helpful, but it would be a bad mistake to suppose that one has made progress simply by having internalized their contents."

Be Honest about All Things

Changing our habits is hard especially if we don't know why we do what we do.

We must learn to be mindful of our urges that keep us from being in the moment, committing, engaging, and showing up. "Why do I feel like this?" Figure it out. Investigate your feelings. Dissect them. If you feel any resistance, this is your cue to keep going. The main challenge is training your brain to think like this.

I'm not talking about some unconscious reflex or talent. Practicing self-awareness is like training a muscle. It gets stronger the more it is used.

The quote of Epicurus' fits very well here: "A consciousness of wrongdoing is the first step to salvation."

Daily Reflection

Do you have a troll that follows you on Instagram? You really shouldn't respond. There is no reason to let them know how to unfollow you. They know. Do you have to respond to that email right now?

In what I have noticed in my own experiences the people who excel in their work, who have mastered their craft, have gotten where they are because they can prioritize. They know what they need to do each hour in their day. If we could film a day in the life of our heroes, how would our focus, work ethic, or determination compare? Would we be able to do the same type of work?

I timed myself on the amount of time I spent looking through Instagram and watching other people. I was shocked at the numbers of hours that had been wasted. Taking a break during the day is fine, but we need to keep in mind how we actually interact with these distractions. Some might even be considered an addiction.

The time we spend swiping our finger across a screen is time that should have been spent creating what others want to see.

People Were Not Created to Procrastinate

When I have a day that I'm having problems getting out of bed, I remember this...

If you don't want to get out of bed, you need to tell yourself: "You must go to work. What is there that I must complain about? If I do what I was meant to do, and what I was created for, why am I huddling under the blankets trying to stay warm?"

Your subconscious mind will say, "It's nice here."

You reply, "Yes, but was I born to just feel nice? I was born to experience and do things. Look at the bees, spiders, ants, birds, and plants. They are doing what they were created to do. You are lying here not wanting to do your part as a human. You should be running to do what nature demands of you.

Your mind rebuts, "We must sleep."

"This is true, but nature has set a limit on sleep just like it has with drinking and eating. You have exceeded your limit on sleep. You have gotten enough. You haven't worked enough yet. You are very far below your quota. You must not love yourself since you are not showing that you love your nature and what it asks of you. The people that love what they do will make themselves weak doing it. They will sometimes forget to stop and eat. You don't have the respect that the social climber has for status, the miser for money, the ballerina for ballet, or the artist for painting. When they have become possessed by their craft, they will stop sleeping or eating before they stop doing their craft."

Lay down Your Phone and Get in the Moment

The problem isn't that we are in a time of distractions but a time where we have failed to embrace and teach ourselves and others to be mindful. A child eating with her family while playing a game on her tablet is the same as an adult checking emails and texts while on a date. Both examples are moments that humans can connect with others. I'm not talking about through their devices. I'm talking about connecting with the people around you. You need to learn to enjoy those around you and communicate with them.

Learning to be alone and present in the moment are both habits we have to learn. Some are better at it than others. These people make an effort to do it. They actually need it or they will go mad.

Try to find some time during the day to just sit and stay still. It can be a few seconds or even minutes. You can be anywhere. Lay down your phone, tablet, whatever it is that is distracting you. Take some deep breaths, and just think about what has happened during your day. While you are working, think about everything you are doing. Focus on it. Focus on what you want to accomplish. You need to do this with care, attentiveness, patience, and diligence. You will eventually realize how this will help you be creative with your craft and help your quality of life.

Seneca said it best, "Nothing, to my way of thinking, is a better proof of a well-ordered mind than a man's ability to stop just where he is and pass some time in his own company."

Time is the Most Valuable Resource

The most challenging thing about Stoicism is death is always in their thoughts. They understand that our lives are fleeting and this gets repeated throughout all aspects of life.

When you stop and think about it, you have lived so many days and hours already and you are not guaranteed any more time in the life you have in front of you. It can make you feel rather anxious. If you truly think about this, you will see that each day is a chance to improve, to learn, to appreciate what you can do. You will see that only you are responsible for your quality of life.

This should make your growth, attention, self-awareness, generosity, work ethic, and self-respect the most important thing in your life. None of us wants to die or even think about death. We don't want to have regrets. This is how Stoicism will help you put purpose in your life. I will humble you and motivate you.

Seneca said it best when he said, "We should hunt out the helpful pieces of teaching and the spirited and noble-minded sayings which are capable of immediate practical application — not far far-fetched or archaic expressions or extravagant metaphors and figures of speech — and learn them so well that words become works."

How we live and complete our crafts must physically show the principles we follow. We need to live, learn, and create more and consume, criticize and compare less.

Chapter 6: The Basic Tenets Of Stoicism (The Three Topoi)

Stoicism has three basic tenets whose practical application of, according to stoic teachings, leads to a life experience that is in tune with nature.

Stoicism offers a unified account of nature. This account consists of the three topoi or basic tenets that are logic (formal), physics (monistic), and ethics (naturalistic). Of these tenets, early stoicism considered ethics more important to human knowledge.

Before we discuss each of the three topoi individually, it is important to mention and point out that although stoics consider ethics important and central to happiness (the experience of), ethics alone is not enough, which is why it needs the support of the other fields of inquiry: logic and physics.

Also worth mentioning and noting is that from the very beginning, the aim of stoicism was to provide a practical philosophy whose practitioners of could apply in their daily lives and in so doing, experience a eudaimonic or happy life, one guided by key virtues.

As stoicism developed through the Roman era, the aim of the philosophy became using the basic tenet of ethics to achieve apatheia, equanimity or a state of mind free from the disturbance of the passions that we will discuss later.

The achievement of equanimity through the practice of cardinal virtue (ethics) required the support of the other two tenets: logic, the theory of knowledge as well as how to reason and think about nature and the world in which we live, and physic, metaphysics, natural science, or the study of the world we live in.

Although individual, the three topoi relate in the following sense. Stoics use the analogy of an egg to show the relationship between the three tenets.

In this sense, logic is the outer shell; ethics is the egg white and physics is the York:

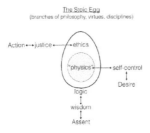

The Stoic Egg
(branches of philosophy, virtues, disciplines)

Action ←→ justice ←—— ← ethics

"physics" ——— → self-control

Desire

logic

wisdom

Assent

The best way to conceptualize the interconnected of the three topoi is to think of a garden. In this case, logic would be the fence protecting the delicate interior; the nutritive soil would be the physics that enriches your knowledge of the world, while the fruits of the planted plants would be the ethics, the intended aim of the stoic practice.

There is no consensus on the sequential order of implementation of the three basic tenets of stoicism. Most philosophers note that for a naturalistic philosophy such as stoicism is that all the pillars are complimentary and important to the practical implementation of the philosophy in one's life.

1: Logic

Early stoics believed that being a sage, someone who practiced virtue and lived in oneness with nature, meant having good knowledge of the world or things. To cultivate formal logic, stoics relied on (and still do) cognitive and moral progress, an idea dubbed prokopê, making progress.

Stoic logic does not hold that all impressions are true; on the contrary, it holds that some impressions lead to comprehension (are cataleptic) while others are not.

Stoicism also admits that perception is not always right and can be wrong, as is the case with phantasma, a term meaning impressions of the mind such as dreams, hallucinations, and other unconscious judgments. The aim of stoic logic is to train, or make gradual progress, towards distinguishing between cataleptic and non-cataleptic impression. Ancient stoics such as Chrysippus maintained that it was important for stoic sages to absorb different forms of impressions as a means to progress.

Stoic logic is about cultivating the ability to distinguish between opinion that is weak or false, apprehension, and knowledge based on firm impression and reason that is beyond alteration or reproach. Stoicism holds that this kind of cataleptic impression is the first step on the ladder to actual knowledge.

Stoic logic is propositional logic, a type of logic concentrated on the validity of arguments rather than the truth per se or logical theorem. The main use of logic in stoicism is to use it to complement ethics and guard against perceptions that may compromise it.

2: Physics

Stoic physics amounts to what we would now refer to as theology, natural science, and metaphysics.

In relation to natural science, the underlying stoic principle is to live "in accordance with nature." This means we should aim to understand nature as best as we can, with its study and comprehension aimed at being complementary to the achievement of a eudaimonic life. Stoicism holds that everything we consider real, i.e. existing, is corporeal but also that some things such as time, void, and sayables are incorporeal.

Ancient stoicism embraced a vitalist understanding of nature governed by two main principles, one active in the form of logos and relating to God and reason, the other passive and relating to matter and substance. The active principle is indestructible while the other took the form of the four elements of fire, water, air, and earth and is therefore destructible to the point of being eternally recurring in nature and the cosmos.

Stoicism notes that the cosmos is alive and guided by a rational principle (logos) called the aether or stoic fire, which is different from elemental fire, the fire we know of and that is capable of burning and destroying.

Stoic logic also notes the immanence of God in the universe, a fact displayed by the creative cosmic fire. Unlike Christianity and Aristotelian, stoicism does not believe in a God who is a prime mover or existing outside space and time; they hold that if that were the case, if God was incorporeal, he would be unable to act on things because according to the philosophy, what is incorporeal lacks causal powers.

A core teaching of stoic physic is that all things have a cause. Chrysippus held that it is impossible for motion to occur without a cause. To this, stoicism holds steadfastly to the notion of universal causality as a branch of its physics and explanation of the nature of the cosmos, which is that nature and the future operate within the laws of physics.

"[The Stoics] say that it is impossible, when all the circumstances surrounding both the cause and that of which it is a cause are the same, that things should not turn out a certain way on one occasion but that they should turn out that way on some other occasion"

Cicero

Ancient stoics also believed that chance is nothing but human ignorance in the sense that chance happens out of events we humans do not understand.

3: Ethics

Like logos and physics, Stoic ethics are less theory and more practical. Stoic ethics is the study you, a stoic, should live your life.

From antiquity, living a life governed by ethics was the aim of the philosophy, a fact that many famous stoics acknowledge as not being easy and therefore requiring prokopê, making progress.

"The philosopher's lecture room is a hospital: you ought not to walk out of it in a state of pleasure, but in pain—for you are not in good condition when you arrive!"

Epictetus

The essense of ethics is the acknowledgment that, as the Enchiridon notes, we have control over some things and no control over others:

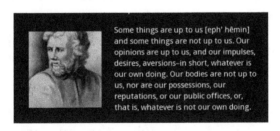

Some things are up to us [eph' hêmin] and some things are not up to us. Our opinions are up to us, and our impulses, desires, aversions–in short, whatever is our own doing. Our bodies are not up to us, nor are our possessions, our reputations, or our public offices, or, that is, whatever is not our own doing.

For early stoics, "live in accordance with nature" was the principle motto in ethics.

With this, they meant that we should live lives that are in tune with nature (the cosmos), and human nature, to which they noted that humans are social beings capable of rational judgment especially in relation to how to live life.

Close to the idea of following human nature was oikeiôsis, another stoic concept that translates to affinity. Stoicism believes that as humans, we have the natural ability to develop morally and that this natural propensities begin instinctually but are refinable as we age and learn how to reason.

The stoic naturalistic account of how we develop virtues or moral behavior is in line with what we know from cognitive science and evolution. For example, we know that by nature, we always act in a manner that advances our interest and goals be they health or wealth related. We also have the ability to identify with the interests of others, and to find practical ways to navigate through life and its many difficulties.

According to stoicism, these propensities have a direct relation with the four cardinal virtues that govern our lives: courage, practical wisdom, temperance, and justice. To pursue our goals, we need courage and temperance; justice is a natural part of being a human existing in a social society where we have a circle of friends or people we interact with daily. On its part, phronêsis, or practical wisdom, gives us the ability to deal with the many circumstances that make up our lives.

In addition to these four cardinal virtues, stoicism notes that because they relate to each other, each of them has major categories. For example, under practical wisdom are the virtues of good judgment, resourcefulness, and discretion; under temperance are the virtues of propriety, self-control, and honor; under courage are the virtues of confidence, magnanimity, and perseverance. Under justice are the values of sociability, kindness, and piety.

Even with the cardinal virtues as derived from Socrates, the stoic understanding of virtue is unitary—pluralism. For instance, justice is practical wisdom applied socially; courage is endurance, and temperance is choice, and as such, all virtues are inseparable—it is impossible to be courageous but not temperate.

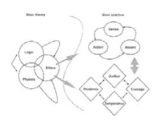

The four cardinal virtues and the three tenets (topoi) that govern stoicism relate greatly to the stoic disciplines of desire, action, and assent that we will discuss in the next chapter and illustrate how to apply in your life in a practical manner.

The aim of stoic ethics is to help you differentiate between the two stoic concepts introduced by Zeno: preferred and dispreferred indifferents.

According to Zeno and stoic teachings, some indifferents have value, axia, while others lack it, apaxia. Axia consists of preferred indifferents such as education, wealth, and health. Apaxia consists of dispreferred conditions such as ignorance, sickness, and poverty.

Although stoicism teaches that some indifferents such as wealth, health, and education are preferred, these indifferents are only preferred when they do not compromise but instead enhance the practice of virtue. Even the preferred indifferents are not truly necessary to experiencing a happy or eudemonic existence.

This means that while it is human nature to seek some preferred conditions such as wealth, better health, and education, as long as you practice the cardinal virtues and the ones underneath them, your happiness, wellness, or wellbeing is independent of these external or material circumstances.

From the onset, stoicism held that understanding nature—or if you may, the cosmos—informs our understanding of ethics, the understanding of how to live a eudemonic life.

Now that you have a basic understanding of the three topoi (or basic tenets) of stoicism, let us look at the disciplines underneath or governing each of the tenets.

Chapter 7: Confronting Your Reality

Sooner or later, everybody needs to manage situations and circumstances which are not perfect. In this life, you'll need to CONFRONT the truth, as is it is the most straightforward thing to do. The fact that you can TOLERATE your present circumstances can make you more joyful in the present and will prompt a better future.

We all reach a point where life gets scary and messy, and we just feel like we can't deal with it anymore. Some of the situations which upset us and drain our effort to deal with reality include: financial difficulties, health issues, child-rearing, relationship problems, conflicts in society, and others. When all of these issues become one big reality, then that is what makes it completely overwhelming and intimidating!

What happens when we are faced with this huge reality? For one, we tend to avoid it. We fail to talk about it or deal with it. We fail to go for medical checkups. We fail to balance or finances. We get stuck in relationships which are messed up. Ultimately, we fail to face our emotional issues.

Instead of facing our reality, we retire from it and resign ourselves to doing other unnecessary things. Hence, we waste our energy on spending hours watching TV, going on Facebook, gossiping with friends, indulging in food and sex, daydreaming all day, and other unhealthy habits. As a result, this takes away our time, energy, and attention, all of which we could have used to confront and deal with our reality. We just let the power and energy slip through our fingers, hoping that one time soon, everything will be okay and we will feel better.

When we involve ourselves in activities which redirect that energy meant for confronting reality, it only makes us feel better for a while. Meanwhile, our problems just keep on piling up and getting bigger, scarier, and messier. Just because you ignore something doesn't mean it goes away; it tends to get worse.

Eventually, it reaches the point when we can no longer ignore our problems. We are forced to deal with them, whether we like it or not. The worst thing about this is that we are already in a crisis mode. We now have so many emergencies to attend to, such as job loss, lingering illness, repossession of property, family crisis, and more.

But then, if we initially made a habit of confronting our problems regularly, we might have been on the safe side; we could have avoided the damage. In the first place, we could have been in a position to prevent all the crises which are now happening.

To CONFRONT your circumstances doesn't mean to like it or to support the conditions that led you there. To confront your reality means to know your part in causing the problem. In order to completely acknowledge a reality, it is critical for you to recognize the part that you played in causing the issue. By identifying the root cause, you can work towards achieving a solution for your own unique reality.

Have you stopped to consider what you might want your life to look like? If you're getting ready for a better future, then it may help when you ACCEPT and CONFRONT the situation you are in at present. If you DEAL with it now, then it can give you something to look forward to later.

Think of it as your duty to deal with the reality. It is a part of your personal care; it is an act of self-love. So, love yourself enough and face your reality better! Below are tips to help you FACE the reality you're in, even when you don't want to:

Take an Honest Assessment of Your Life

The first step to starting an honest SELF-ASSESSMENT is to make time for it. Have some time for yourself. Use this time alone to practice activities that relax your body and mind.

Next, get a notebook and write down the main areas of your life. These include Family, Health, Wealth, and Work. Now make a separate page for each of these. Write down the current situation with each of them.

On each of these areas, write down what is working and what is not. Look at those things which are going well and why they're going well. Reflect on what you've done to make these areas turn out well. On the other hand, look at those things which are not going well or as expected. What have you done to improve the situation? What other efforts can you add to help the situation? Which situations are most important? Which ones are most urgent?

After all of these reflections, you'll be able to see what really disturbs you in life. Remember that you are not after perfection; nothing is perfect in life. The self-reflection is about being aware of your situation and seeing what is within your power to change or improve. Also, it is about being able to make plans and preparations, so that you don't fall helplessly into situations, purely by surprise.

Look at Your Regular Exit Mechanisms

Simply put, EXIT MECHANISMS are your way of escaping from reality. Escaping from a situation makes us have a temporary, good feeling. However, it reaches a time when you cannot run away anymore from the situation you are facing. All you have done is delayed and lengthened the process – if not, worsened it.

Thus, early on, it helps to realize what your regular exit MECHANISMS are. What distracts you from doing what you are supposed to do? Do you go out and find something else to do, when you should be doing your chores or having that talk? Do you call in sick and stay in bed, as your way of missing a meeting or sleeping in on a Monday?

Next, learn how to deal with these DISTRACTIONS. As a simple example, set you alarm so you can wake up early. Distance your alarm clock, so you'd have to get up to turn it off. Stay in and finish your stuff first, before you go out and leave to have some fun. In short, just get things done. Come to realize that seeking pleasure instead of dealing with your situation (or handling your obligations) is a form of exit. It's an escape mechanism that tends to backfire in the end.

After you've identified the mechanisms you use to exit and the distractions you use as an excuse, think in terms of FREQUENCY. Keep track of how many times in a day (or a week) that you've tried to escape. Is this the second time you've been late for work this week? Have you tried three times to get your report done today, only to drift off into your iPhone or your iPod? Have you lost count of the number of times you were supposed to meet up and talk?

Look at how many times it's been that you knew you should be doing something, but you couldn't seem to face it. Look for what it is exactly that you've been trying to avoid this number of times. This can be an eye-opening experience.

Draft Your New Realities

Let's admit it. If you're new to it, the idea of facing your reality can be so scary that it makes you feel anxious and helpless. You don't have to remain in these states of anxiety and helplessness. Instead, figure out what you need to do next. Maybe you need to change your behavior, devise a plan, or use your time more wisely. It is CHANGE which comes first, before you can create a new reality.

In line with drafting your new reality, it helps to come up with a PLAN and to write it down. First, set the new goals which you want to achieve. List down the changes which need to get done, and prioritize those tasks which are most urgent and important to you.

Next, put your plan into ACTION. Try hard to work first on those things which are of value and importance to you in your life. Also, resist the urge to procrastinate things which you know, if you fail to fulfill, might bring about unavoidable consequences.

Even when you've accomplished something, continue to set new GOALS. In this way, you'll be able to shift your mindset towards focusing on the newly-set plan and anticipating the outcome of your new goals.

In the meantime, do away with negative THOUGHTS. Use the approach of replacing negative thoughts with positive ones. This practice will enable you to face your reality while, at the same time, improving your outlook and making you feel better.

When you're feeling down, overpowered, furious, or simply disappointed, then turn to the practice of SELF-ALLEVIATING techniques. A vital technique in dealing with your feelings on an everyday basis, its practice allows you to adapt to the feelings by utilizing self-calming strategies. Usually, it is yoga, meditation, aromatherapy, and massage which work for some people. What's important is that you identify self-relieving exercises that work for you and apply them whenever necessary.

Seek Help When Needed

Have you thought about seeking help? When you're too overwhelmed by your life, you could approach an accountability partner, a coach, or a therapist to help you devise plans that confront your reality. These individuals would understand what you're going through and will enable you to stick to your plans.

When you arrange for help and find it, it will allow you to achieve your objective.

You'll be guided on how to break down your main objective (dealing with that one huge reality) into smaller sections (facing the many, little realities of life), and this makes problems easier to solve. Thus, by facing one problem at a time, you'd be able to manage those circumstances in life which used to overwhelm and disturb you.

Since the whole idea of facing your reality is for you to move on, it also calls on you to leave your comfort zone. You need to love yourself and your life enough to try and make the situation different. This is your responsibility, and no one can do it better than yourself.

To wrap it up: Devise a plan, with goals to achieve. Set clear goals and know where you are going. Clear away those distractions and use your time wisely. In time, you'll have dealt with all your immediate problems, and it will become much easier for you to face the next realities which come your way.

Chapter 8: The Lives Of Ancient Stoics

If you're thinking of making a lifestyle change from extreme to moderate, then no one expects you to make it happen overnight. As with everything in life, it is one of those things that take practice and time. Like we've said, it often takes the rest of our lives to learn to control our passions and live in moderation.

In this section, we are not looking for perfect examples of prominent people who have mastered their emotions. Rather, we are turning to their lives as an example how Stoicism was applied and what basic traits of a Stoic they best exemplified. Briefly, let's get a glimpse of how the ancient Stoics lived.

How Epictetus Lived

From his humble beginnings to his fame as a teacher of philosophy, Epictetus was one of the earliest examples of a Stoic. Born a slave in Hierapolis (now Pamukkale in Turkey) in 55 A.D., he had such an interest in philosophy that his owner permitted him to study under master philosopher, Gaius Musonius Rufus. All these happened at a time when Rome was ruled by a cruel, tyrannical emperor we now know of as Nero.

After Nero's death, Epictetus started teaching philosophy in Rome. His teachings reached Greece, and it was here in Nicopolis where he founded a school on Stoic philosophy, with one of his students being a future emperor of Rome in the person of Marcus Aurelius.

Although many of the ancient texts of his time did not survive, we refer to the writings of Epictetus in his book, "Discourses", for a better glimpse into his life. (Note: Studies show that it would be hard to tell whether most of the content was written by Epictetus, or by his student, Flavius Arrian.)

In "Discourses", Epictetus discussed a variety of philosophical topics ranging from fear and friendship, to illness and poverty. He talked about how to keep tranquil and why not to be angry with other people.

This strikes a chord as, back when he had been enslaved, he was said to have been tortured by his master. This resulted in his suffering from a broken leg. From that time on, he was lame for the rest of his life.

With anger as our example, Epictetus cites that when a Stoic (prokoptôn) is treated unfairly by his brother, he should not respond with angry indignation. This is contrary to the nature of brothers, for brothers must act right towards each other.

Metaphorically, he often spoke of his school as a hospital where students came to be treated for their illnesses. Like the rest of humans living in society, they were beset by anxieties, frustrations, and setbacks in life. In spite of these difficulties, they were rewarded with the blessing of relationships, transient as these were.

According to Epictetus, we suffer from ills as a result of a mistaken belief in what is truly good. People tend to invest their hope in the wrong thing, if not in the wrong way. Thus, the teachings of Epictetus remind us to invest our hope in that which will truly bring us lasting happiness (or Eudaimonia).

In the face of misfortune and disappointment, he also exhorts us to practice removing cries and laments of "Alas" or "Poor me" when we suffer.

Instead, we must understand what is "in our power" or what is "up to us".

"Sickness is a hindrance to the body, but not to your ability to choose, unless that is your choice. Lameness is a hindrance to the leg, but not to your ability to choose. Say this to yourself with regard to everything that happens, then you will see such obstacles as hindrances to something else, but not to yourself."

- Epictetus

How Marcus Aurelius Lived

As for Marcus Aurelius, credit goes to his teacher, Junius Rusticus, for introducing him to Epictetus. Born in 121 A.D., Marcus Aurelius is recognized as one of the greatest Roman emperors who ever ruled and lived. In it said that, during a lull in one of his war campaigns, he was able to write a private journal which eventually became public.

With his work compiled into a book called "Meditations", he wrote about subjects such as self-awareness, humility, service, death, and nature. These reflections serve as reminders on Stoic principles which can be applied during times of challenge and hardship.

Don't forget that, at the time he was a Roman emperor, emperors then were practically considered as deity. This did not stop him, however, from writing about subject like humility and service, as mentioned.

To him, Stoicism was not one big instruction manual (or a "grand instructor" as he called it), but a soothing balm which lends comfort to us whenever we suffer injury.

At every hour, give your full concentration, as a Roman and a man, to carrying out the task in hand with a scrupulous and unaffected dignity and affectionate concern for others and freedom and justice, and give yourself space from all other concerns. (2) You will give yourself this if you carry out each act as if it were the last of your life, freed from all randomness and passionate deviation from the rule of reason and from pretense and self-love and dissatisfaction with what has been allotted to you. (3) You see how few things you need to master to be able to live a smoothly flowing and god-fearing life; the gods will ask no more from someone who maintains these principles. (2.5, trans. Gill)

- Marcus Aurelius, "Meditations"

How Seneca Lived

A first-century philosopher, Lucius Annaeus Seneca or simply Seneca the Younger was one of the most famous philosophers of his time. Successful and wealthy, he was a powerful man and a political adviser of Nero.

One of the thoughts which Seneca is admired for was his perspective on misfortune. In principle, he believed not only in thinking about misfortune, but also in living it. Thus, for a set number of days per month, he used to practice poverty. Basically, this meant having only a little amount of food, wearing the worst possible clothes, and being away from a good bed and from all the comforts of home. Allowing himself to come face-to-face with being in a state of want, he would then ask himself: "Is this what I used to dread?"

In this practice of misfortune, it was not that he was afraid of losing something or that he anticipated suffering from misfortune. Rather, it was more in order for suffering to lose its ability to upset him and disrupt the balance of his life.

As a Stoic, Seneca believed that anger was more than an irrational outburst, over which we seemingly had no control. Instead, he regarded it as a philosophical problem which could be solved and treated. According to Senecan thought, anger arose from being overly optimistic about the world. In turn, this over-optimism led to unrealistic expectations which could hardly be met. If one were more mentally prepared for such unexpected events, perhaps, with a more pessimistic attitude, one could manage to accept the results without manifesting outbursts of anger.

When Nero turned on Seneca and betrayed him, the former asked the latter to commit suicide. In the face of this terrible ordeal, all Seneca could think of was how to comfort his family (particularly his wife) and his friends.

"It is in times of security that the spirit should be preparing itself for difficult times; while fortune is bestowing favors on it is then is the time for it to be strengthened against her rebuffs."

Seneca

How Cato the Younger Lived

Marcus Porcius Cato Uticensis, or better known as Cato the Younger, was famous as a Stoic orator and philosopher. Disliked for who he was in history, many writers argue on whether or not Cato should be added to the roster of ancient Stoics. This, however, is about how he lived.

One thing which this statesman and politician is remembered for would be his stubbornness. Stubborn and tenacious as he was, his peers learned to respect him at a young age. Those who knew him well suppose that he was feared, more than he was hated. Firm in his republican beliefs, he grew up to become a leader in the late Roman Republic.

In all likelihood, his lack of popularity sprung in part from his constant opposition of the great Roman emperor, Julius Caesar, and the rest of the triumvirate. It is said that he ran once for office on an honest, unscrupulous campaign, but lost to opponents who were less conscientious. This was at a time when electoral fraud and bribery were so rampant.

Both admired and shunned for his honesty, he refused to participate in extortion, did an honest accounting, and tried to maintain an untainted reputation. Although he was offered the prestigious position of praetorship, he again refused this and regarded it as an unlawful honor.

Honest yet stubborn to a fault, Cato's life ended in a tragedy. Unwilling to submit to Caesar, he took his own life and, thus, ironically tainted what would have been a remarkably clean record of living as a Stoic.

Chapter 9: Preparing For The Practice Of Stoicism

STOICISM ITSELF INVOLVES many practices that allow you to engage in Stoicism during various times in your life. Each practice, however, requires you to engage in a certain level of authenticity, mindfulness, discipline, and humility in order for you to effectively engage in that practice. Before you begin overwhelming yourself with the practices of Stoicism, it can be useful to prepare yourself for the practice of Stoicism. This way, you are equipped with all of the necessary tools to help you experience Stoicism in a more deep and meaningful manner.

You can consider this act of preparation as an opportunity for you to prime your mindset for what Stoicism will demand out of you. This is your opportunity to start viewing Stoicism in a more accurate and meaningful way so that when you begin to embrace the acts, you are not merely learning about them, but you are truly embracing them in your life. For many, the transition from knowing into doing can be fairly challenging. If it is not embraced, however, you are unlikely to gain any benefit from Stoicism because you will not truly be living the values of the Stoic way.

Embrace Your Authentic Self

Our society is built in a way that often defies our need to embrace our authentic self and live as the truest expression of who we are. In many cases, people are bullied and punished out of being who they are, rather than encouraged to explore more of their authentic self and embrace that self wholly. Alas, this pressure we experience from society to abandon our authentic self is something that is beyond our control, and therefore, we should not waste our time trying to stop it or trying to create the perfect conditions to be authentic. The more you try to control the world around you so that it is safe to be you, the longer you are going to wait to express as your true self.

Instead of waiting for the conditions to be perfect, choose to show up as yourself anyway. Practice being indifferent to what other people think or feel about how you are showing up. Allow yourself to show up anyway, trusting that you judge your authentic expression as being a positive and fulfilling thing and that this judgment is the only one that matters.

As you begin to embrace your authentic self, you may realize that the disconnect you experienced as a result of the pressures of the world around you makes it somewhat challenging for you to do this. You might realize that you were drawn further away from authentic expression than you realized, and you may even find yourself struggling to identify what your authentic expression even is. The best way to embrace your authentic expression is to practice being the most authentic version of yourself possible in each moment and trust that the more authentic you are, the more you will uncover who your authentic self even is.

The more you practice being your authentic self, the more opportunities you are going to have to witness other people's opinions of your authentic self (stimulus), and the more you are going to have the opportunity to choose your response to those opinions (judgment and voluntary action.) It can be challenging to move away from your knee-jerk reaction of feeling intimidated, embarrassed, guilty, or anxious anytime someone has an opinion of you that does not feel good. However, the more you choose to see that opinion as having nothing to do with you and being irrelevant to your self-expression, the more you will find yourself feeling confident and developing a greater resiliency toward the world around you. As this skill continues to grow, you will find that you begin to feel more at peace with your life experiences and that you no longer feel so phased by other people's opinions of who you are. This also begins to develop your feelings of integrity and the sense of wholeness you experience when you choose to express as your authentic self in life.

Be Mindful

Mindfulness is at the core of Stoicism as it gives you the opportunity to cultivate your reason and develop your self-awareness, as well as your greater awareness. As you prepare to embrace a more Stoic lifestyle and mindset, learn how to be more mindful about yourself and the world around you. Through this, you are going to increase your time spent in the gap between stimulus and reaction, making it easier for you to carefully choose your judgment and your action. You will also find yourself naturally leaning toward a more resilient, confident, and calm life experience as you begin to notice the opportunity to take greater responsibility for and control over yourself.

Developing mindfulness is a life-long process that requires daily practice and effort if you are going to be able to truly develop a mindful state. You must be willing to continually practice checking in with yourself and your experience and making sure that your interpretation and awareness of the world around you is accurate and aligns with the truth, as well as the highest good of all. The more you can check in with yourself, the easier it will become to check in with yourself and notice your feelings, thoughts, and experiences. You will also begin to expand your mindfulness from mindful check-ins to a more constant state of mindfulness.

Of course, just like the Stoic teachers themselves preached, you will never reach a state where you are completely mindful all the time. After all, we are only human, and it is within our nature and reason to believe that we are going to experience mistakes and that at times we are going to give in to our primal instincts over our reasonable ones. Remember, the goal with Stoicism is not to become perfect or to transcend our human tendencies and emotions. Our goal is to work toward offsetting at least a few of our own wrongdoings so that we can experience a greater and more fulfilling life.

A great way to begin developing your mindfulness right now is to set an alarm in your phone that reminds you that it is time to check in with yourself at various points throughout the day. When that alarm goes off, pause and reflect on your thoughts and your emotions. Notice how your body feels, if you have any needs that are going unmet, or if there is anything that may be preventing you from feeling positive and well in that moment. Also, take a moment to notice and appreciate anything that is feeling good or going in your favor in that moment. Drop into your senses and notice what you see, taste, smell, feel, and hear. Give yourself this moment to spend with your body and to really mindfully become aware of your experience. As you continue doing this, you will find yourself naturally increasing your awareness of the world around you and, as a result, creating the perfect opportunity for you to improve your Stoic practices later on!

Boost Your Self-Discipline

Any change you make in your life will always be temporary if you lack self-discipline. To experience true, lasting change in your life, you must be disciplined enough to continually work toward integrating that change until you get the results you desire. Although discipline is something we experience all throughout our lives, the discipline we experience is generally from other people trying to discipline us to behave in the ways they want us to behave. This can draw away from your ability to experience life as your authentic self while taking responsibility over your life experiences.

Developing your self-discipline can be done over a series of different practices. You can start by getting to know your strengths and weaknesses so that you can start creating practical means for offsetting your weaknesses and reinforcing your strengths. Another way you can increase your self-discipline is by recognizing what temptations are for you and eliminating these temptations from your life so that you can focus more exclusively on what needs to get done. If completely eliminating a certain temptation from your life is not feasible, you can always create stronger boundaries around that temptation so that it distracts you less.

As you begin to flex your self-discipline muscle, you will find that it becomes easier for you to increase your sense of self-discipline over time. It will also become easier for you to start relying on self-discipline to support you with creating healthier habits, a greater sense of detachment from that which you cannot control, and a deeper ability to embrace all that Stoicism has to offer you.

Stay Humble

One great way to deepen your Stoic abilities is to create the capacity to stay humble. Humbleness shields us from the rises and falls that intense pride can create for us. When you experience a heightened sense of pride or ego, you might find yourself feeling particularly arrogant about your ability to remain detached, balanced, and Stoic. Often, you can tell that you are in this sense of pride and ego because you will find yourself feeling as though you are "the best" at being Stoic, or like you "cannot possibly make any mistakes." These types of beliefs lead to you feeling a possibly quiet yet intensely deep sense of attachment to your balance, resulting in you feeling particularly shaken when you make a mistake or when life knocks you down.

Humbleness is not about denying your feelings, nor is it really about your feelings at all. Instead, humbleness is choosing to be of the mindset that anything could happen, good or bad, and that it could affect you in any number of ways. Having the awareness that you are not better than, or more protected than, anyone else on this earth enables you to remain humble. Through this, you exude far less arrogance, and you are much less ignorant toward the reality of hardships both in your own life and in the lives of others. You will also find yourself having a far more balanced frame of mind when it comes to facing any unexpected hardships because you will not be caught in the inaccurate mindset of "it could not happen to me."

You can increase your sense of humbleness by recognizing that anyone could experience anything at any time, including you. Work toward blurring the lines between yourself and others, realizing that their misfortune could just as easily be yours, and yours theirs. Have compassion when any of you go through hardships, and be kind in the way that you act toward others. When you embrace the mindset and behavior of humbleness, you prepare yourself greatly to embrace the true power of Stoicism.

Chapter 10: How To Practice Mindfulness

Importance of gratitude in our lives

Stoicism teaches and encourages the value of gratitude. This gratitude is not just limited to material wealth and blessings, but it also involves time. As according to Marcus Aurelius, "Be happy for this moment. This moment is your life." He also wrote, "When you arise in the morning, think of what a precious privilege it is to be alive --- to breathe, to think, to enjoy, to love." Gratitude is very important and the benefits of experiencing it are remarkable.
Exercise: Gratitude Journal

Start your personal gratitude journal.

Write down at least three things that went well during the day.

Shortly describe the causes and give a casual explanation for every good thing.

Do this every night.

Once a week go through your journal and experience the appreciation. Try to keep this feeling as long as possible.

Tip:

For better results do it before going to sleep. Thanks to that, the feeling of gratitude will resonate for the whole next day.

Exercise: Personal Gratitude Jar

Find any empty jar and place it in the visible part of your apartment or work place. The placing is very important, it has to remind you to do the next steps.

Put a label on it with a visible inscription "I am grateful" or something that will inspire you.

Now, every time when you fill grateful for something put a small amount of money.

When the jar will get full, donate the money to someone. This way you will share your gratefulness with others.

Of course, there are times when practicing gratitude can be a challenge. This is true, especially once you compare yourself with others who "have more in life." However, the Stoics discourage such kind of comparison and teach that you should not envy about the things that you do not have --- for such things there is no end. As written by Seneca to a friend: "In all things, we should try to make ourselves be as grateful as possible."

Here is a great technic that will help you to appreciate what you already have: Technic #1

Think of Those Who Have Less

You already compared yourself to those who "have more in life", but now try to compare to those who have less or nothing. Maybe, it is someone you know or a homeless person you see on the street every time you go to work. Think what life is for them. Think of people with disabilities and how they have to face everyday reality or children who were sold by their parents to slavery for some drugs. But do not get depressed by the fates of those people, rather admire their strengths and appreciate what you have and never complain.

Technic #2

Help Others

Stoicism encourages a cheerful spirit. Its teachings not to end with just being thankful, but it is also very important to encourage others to live their life to the fullest, to do good and live a virtuous life. Again, never put yourself higher over other people, rather help and inspire them to get better.

How to accept our own faults

I hope you are already hooked to Stoicism and its teachings or at least interested. However, you should be warned that living this way is not as easy as it might look. In fact, the chances are that even if you are well aware of all the pieces of wisdom shared in this book, you may have some challenge putting them all into practice. But this is the whole point. Only when you actually start to implement the teachings and do all the exercises and technics and practice it everyday, then you will see true results. However, do not let failures discourage you. It is, after all, normal for humans to commit faults and mistakes in life. The important thing is to do your best to live a good and virtuous life. Do not be hard on yourself. Accept your faults if you commit any, and give yourself as many chances as you need until you finally master a particular virtue.

Here is a remarkable teaching by Epictetus:

"Remember, it is not enough to be hit or insulted to be harmed, you must believe that you are being harmed. If someone succeeds in provoking you, realize that your mind is complicit in the provocation. Which is why it is essential that we do not respond impulsively to impressions; take a moment before reacting, and you will find it easier to maintain control."

Technic #1

Accept Your Weaknesses

Accept your weaknesses and never stop doing your best to be a better person. In fact, failures or faults are a normal part of development. In a letter sent by Seneca to his older brother, he wrote: "What bad habit did I curb today? How am I better? Were my actions just? How can I improve?" This is something that Seneca admitted that he borrowed from another philosopher. He advised his brother to ask this kind of questions to himself every night and reflect on it.

Once you accept your bad habits and mistakes, you should then reflect on them and think of how you can be a better person. The more open and honest you are with yourself, the better. Of course, before you can accept your own faults, you need to be mindful of yourself. It is not uncommon to find people who do not realize that they have bad habits. This is due to lack of introspection. That is why you need to learn to pay attention to yourself.

Exercise: Self-Examination

Close your eyes.

Take one deep breath and continue to breath normally. However, focus on your breathing.

Become aware of your body and the processes inside of it.

Now focus on what holds you back in achieving your goal. Find your weaknesses.

This step is very important -- accept them.

Think of what you can do to improve them right now.

Open your eyes and keep those thoughts in mind.

Both Seneca and Marcus Aurelius gave this recommendation. Self-examination is important so that you will be aware of any faults that you can remove, as well as habits that you can still improve.

Learning how to be virtuous

True Stoics hold virtue in high regard. It is important to note that virtue is different from knowledge. Knowledge lies in the mind, while virtue expresses itself through actions. Hence, "If you didn't learn these things in order to demonstrate them in practice, what did you learn them for?" There is no quick and easy way to be virtuous. The only way to live a life of virtue is to constantly practice the teachings of Stoicism, which are all rich in virtue and wisdom. Needless to say, knowing these teachings requires continuous study and reflection. The Stoics, believe that living a virtues life is the key to happiness.

To be virtuous means to be mindful not only of yourself but also of the people around you. Be cautious of the trap of being too self-centered. Unfortunately, there are many people who claim to be

Stoics but end up being too narcissistic. Do not think of yourself to be on a higher level than others just because you practice Stoicism or any other philosophy. Do not forget that even those who have no knowledge of philosophy can possess the greatest virtue. Do not be like those who are too egotistical. Stoicism teaches wisdom and humility, not egocentrism. Lets Summarize the Chapter:

Remember to practice gratitude, it is very important and the benefits of experiencing it are remarkable. Make a gratitude Journal or personal gratitude jar.

You should not envy about the things that you do not have --- for such things there is no end. As written by Seneca: "In all things, we should try to make ourselves be as grateful as possible."

Appreciate what you already have. Don`t compare yourself to other, but think of those who have less.

Always help others. Do not end with just being thankful, but also encourage others to live their life to the fullest. Again, never put yourself higher over other people, rather help and inspire them to get better

Realize that living this way is not as easy as it might look. But it is worth it.

Remember to actually start implementing the teachings and do all the exercises and technics and practice them everyday.

Do not let failures discourage you.

Accept your weaknesses, and never stop doing your best to be a better person. You need to learn to pay attention to yourself.

Practice self-examination. It is important, because you will be aware of any faults that you can remove, as well as habits that you can still improve.

Virtue is different from knowledge. Knowledge lies in the mind, while virtue expresses itself through actions. There is no quick and easy way to be virtuous. The only way to live a life of virtue is to constantly practice the teachings of Stoicism.

Be cautious of the trap of being too self-centered. Remember, even those who have no knowledge of philosophy can possess the greatest virtue.

Chapter 11: Stoicism And Indifference

First of all, there is an overgeneralized preconception that stoicism is blandness, dryness, and even something close to frigidity. This couldn't be farther from the truth. Essentially being stoic means aspiring to a calm, unshakeable attitude in front of negative feelings and destructive passions. Stoics don't really praise indifference for its own sake. That would equal a poverty of human experience, inner emptiness, and impaired interpersonal relationships. A stoic attitude welcomes positive emotions and an ability to enjoy happiness or experience joy for very good reasons. However, stoics knew well life is not always so bright and they wanted to have control over bad things and aspects of life as well as over themselves.

Actually, stoicism holds happiness as its primary goal. That's what it promises and can deliver – if you know how to wisely incorporate it in your life. Thus, indifference is only a path to happiness, not a goal in itself. Indifference to malice, misfortune, insults etc. is a sure way of staying happy and in control. Stoicism doesn't advocate a grim, passive, or sterile life. On the contrary, it aims at sparing you all the harmful and consuming feelings that may engulf you unless you deliberately practice a psychology of indifference. Remember that indifference is something a stoic aspires to. They don't start from such an inner reality. The stoic model is one that targets self-control rather than a barren life. In fact, the stoic experiences a feeling of elation each time they manage to control a dangerous emotion or an unwanted external influence through cultivating indifference. As such, indifference can be a path to more pleasant and useful feelings. Keep in mind that stoicism comes down to learned indifference.

Indifference is meant to ensure a desirable state of tranquility that is absolutely necessary for an efficient and successful life regardless of the century people live in. That's why stoicism remains such a valid and valuable life philosophy. It is not necessarily indifference that is a stoic virtue. Indifference is only a means to an end. The real virtues are strength, serenity, and a rational, objective way of perceiving the world as well as the self.

Another important aspect are the ethical implications of stoicism. Let's not forget this philosophy has a very prominent ethical focus. It centered on commitment to truth, grim endurance of opposition or hardship for the sake of one's ideas of right and wrong, and an avoidance of 'bad' emotions and passions (such as envy, greed, rage, hatred, vengefulness etc.). However, it's interesting to notice that stoicism didn't necessarily invoke an external authority (such as a deity) to deal with moral issues. Its point was that people should practice such things for the sake of other important virtues whose effects have clear ethical implications. It was out of genuine commitment to values and belief in what is right that you should do certain things, not because you fear some divine punishment. In this case ...how could stoicism really mean indifference?

An ethical stance is the opposite of indifference. Stoicism doesn't mean permitting evil or not caring about what is right and wrong. Quite the opposite: stoicism highlights the concept of virtue which has prominent ethical implications. However, the ethical content of this doctrine is a highly personalized and interesting take. The bottom line is avoiding dangerous passions, negative emotionality, and entanglements that could bring you under the control of other people. It's as if all other moral values derived from such basic principles. And that is not insignificant at all.

Chapter 12: Cognitive Behavioral Therapy - Stoicism And Medication

First of all, Social Anxiety Disorder/Social Phobia, is the fear, or at least the feeling of discomfort, of being around other people. That's the explanation of the illness in its broadest sense. There are many other particular phobias related to Social Anxiety Disorder, (S.A.D.), but our concern in this article is to look at the various, acceptable treatments available.

The first answer is psychotherapy, and the first method in this respect is Cognitive Behavioral Therapy. I know we've discussed this before, but I want to come at it from a slightly different angle and explain why it's so efficacious and far quicker in showing results than other forms of therapy. There are two main reasons.

Firstly, when the psychiatrist and the patient meet for the first time, they come to a joint decision as to how long the treatment will last. So straightaway they set a goal. It's been found that the average number of sessions a patient has with CBT is sixteen.

Secondly, compare this to psychoanalysis, which may take years.

CBT is a fairly intense, instructive programme, on the other hand, and relies in no small part on homework. The patient must do his or her part for the therapy to prove properly successful. Assuming that the sessions are weekly, then at the end of each session, the patient has certain exercises to do to prepare herself for her next session. Unlike so many other forms of therapy, therefore, the course of treatment is not open-ended.

Thirdly, some practitioners follow the old stoic line of treatment. Basically, this states that if you have a problem, you have one problem. Then you start worrying and fretting over this problem. Now, you have two problems. The trick is to simply accept this problem calmly and work it out. Don't sit around worrying about it. Do something. Fretting isn't doing anything, except digging you deeper and deeper into a ditch from which eventually there could be no escape.

The first thing a psychotherapist should do is to assure the patient that she has no chance of recovering from S.A.D. or any anxiety-based condition by her willpower. How many times have we heard; "Oh, come on, snap out of it." Or; "Suck it up. We all have problems." Patients should be disabused of this thinking right from the word 'go.'

I know that in the past, I've said that I'm no lover of medications. What these drugs are going to do to you in the long term is still largely unknown. This is particularly valid, when you consider that different drugs suit different people. It isn't a case of 'one size fits all.' That being said, however, if a person is suffering acutely, perhaps close to suicide, such is their state of mind, then some form of drug must be administered to calm them down.

The three main types are Anxiolytics, Beta blockers and Antidepressants. Anxiolytics come in the forms of Alprazolam, known as Xanax. Clonazepam, or Klonopin and Diazepam or Valium. Antidepressants we can name next. These come in the forms of Sertraline, which is Zoloft. Bupropion, which is Wellbutrin and Duloxetine, the name for Cymbalta.

Beta blockers are the third type, and are mainly used in cases of cardiac arrhythmias and hypertension. Nevertheless, certain types have proved very useful in the treatment of anxiety disorders. First among these is Propranolol, invented by Sir James Black in the late 50's. Other examples of Beta-blockers are Esmolol, Atenolol and Acebutolol.

I know I've said it before, but it can't be said enough. What works for one person, won't necessarily work for another. Make certain, with the help of your doctor, that both you and the drug he prescribes are in agreement. Some people go for months on a drug that isn't doing them the slightest bit of good, indeed often just the opposite, just because the doctor thought it might help. He or she has to be guided by the patient. If the drug doesn't work, find one that suits you

THE BASICS OF COGNITIVE-BEHAVIORAL THERAPY

Cognitive-Behavioral Therapy is a form of psychotherapy that emphasizes the important role of thinking in how we feel and what we do.

Cognitive-behavioral therapy does not exist as a distinct therapeutic technique. The term "cognitive-behavioral therapy (CBT)" is a very general term for a classification of therapies with similarities. There are several approaches to cognitive-behavioral therapy, including Rational Emotive Behavior Therapy, Rational Behavior Therapy, Rational Living Therapy, Cognitive Therapy, and Dialectic Behavior Therapy.

However, most cognitive-behavioral therapies have the following characteristics:

1. CBT is based on the Cognitive Model of Emotional Response.

Cognitive-behavioral therapy is based on the idea that our thoughts cause our feelings and behaviors, not external things, like people, situations, and events. The benefit of this fact is that we can change the way we think to feel / act better even if the situation does not change.

2. CBT is Briefer and Time-Limited.

Cognitive-behavioral therapy is considered among the most rapid in terms of results obtained. The average number of sessions clients receive (across all types of problems and approaches to CBT) is only 16. Other forms of therapy, like psychoanalysis,can take years. What enables CBT to be briefer is its highly instructive nature and the fact that it makes use of homework assignments. CBT is time-limited in that we help clients understand at the very beginning of the therapy process that there will be a point when the formal therapy will end. The ending of the formal therapy is a decision made by the therapist and client. Therefore, CBT is not an open-ended, never-ending process.

3. A sound therapeutic relationship is necessary for effective therapy, but not the focus. Some forms of therapy assume that the main reason people get better in therapy is because of the positive relationship between the therapist and client. Cognitive-behavioral therapists believe it is important to have a good, trusting relationship, but that is not enough. CBT therapists believe that the clients change because they learn how to think differently and they act on that learning. Therefore, CBT therapists focus on teaching rational self-counseling skills.

4. CBT is a collaborative effort between the therapist and the client.

Cognitive-behavioral therapists seek to learn what their clients want out of life (their goals) and then help their clients achieve those goals. The therapist's role is to listen, teach, and encourage, while the client's roles is to express concerns, learn, and implement that learning.

5. CBT is based on stoic philosophy.

Not all approaches to CBT emphasize stoicism. Rational Emotive Behavior Therapy, Rational Behavior Therapy, and Rational Living Therapy emphasize stoicism. Beck's Cognitive Therapy is not based on stoicism. Cognitive-behavioral therapy does not tell people how they should feel. However, most people seeking therapy do not want to feel they way they have been feeling. The approaches that emphasize stoicism teaches the benefits of feeling, at worst, calm when confronted with undesirable situations. They also emphasize the fact that we have our undesirable situations whether we are upset about them or not. If we are upset about our problems, we have two problems -- the problem, and our upset about it. Most people want to have the fewest number of problems possible. So when we learn how to more calmly accept a personal problem, not only do we feel better, but we usually put ourselves in a better position to make use of our intelligence, knowledge, energy, and resources to resolve the problem.

6. CBT uses the Socratic Method.

Cognitive-behavioral therapists want to gain a very good understanding of their clients' concerns. That's why they often ask questions. They also encourage their clients to ask questions of themselves, like, "How do I really know that those people are laughing at me?" "Could they be laughing about something else?"

7. CBT is structured and directive.

Cognitive-behavioral therapists have a specific agenda for each session. Specific techniques / concepts are taught during each session. CBT focuses on the client's goals. We do not tell our clients what their goals "should" be, or what they "should" tolerate. We are directive in the sense that we show our clients how to think and behave in ways to obtain what they want. Therefore, CBT therapists do not tell their clients what to do -- rather, they teach their clients how to do.

8. CBT is based on an educational model.

CBT is based on the scientifically supported assumption that most emotional and behavioral reactions are learned. Therefore, the goal of therapy is to help clients unlearn their unwanted reactions and to learn a new way of reacting. Therefore, CBT has nothing to do with "just talking". People can "just talk" with anyone. The educational emphasis of CBT has an additional benefit -- it leads to long term results. When people understand how and why they are doing well, they know what to do to continue doing well.

9. CBT theory and techniques rely on the Inductive Method.

A central aspect of Rational thinking is that it is based on fact. Often, we upset ourselves about things when, in fact, the situation isn't like we think it is. If we knew that, we would not waste our time upsetting ourselves. Therefore, the inductive method encourages us to look at our thoughts as being hypotheses or guesses that can be questioned and tested. If we find that our hypotheses are incorrect (because we have new information), then we can change our thinking to be in line with how the situation really is.

10. Homework is a central feature of CBT.

If when you attempted to learn your multiplication tables you spent only one hour per week studying them, you might still be wondering what 5 X 5 equals. You very likely spent a great deal of time at home studying your multiplication tables, maybe with flashcards. The same is the case with psychotherapy. Goal achievement (if obtained) could take a very long time if all a person were only to think about the techniques and topics taught was for one hour per week. That's why CBT therapists assign reading assignments and encourage their clients to practice the techniques learned.

Chapter 13: What Others Think Of Stoicism

Despite all that I've said so far, it's not all sunshine and rainbows. Stoicism isn't perfect, especially when put into practice, and in this chapter, we'll be looking precisely at that. We'll be diving in deep at the struggles one might have while attaining a Stoic mindset, after all, it's easy to talk about accepting grief, but a whole other thing to actually do it.

Furthermore, let's not pretend that Stoicism is the end of all philosophy, there's a lot of philosophies out there, and many of them have fairly good critiques of Stoicism, some of which are positive, and some which aren't quite so. In this chapter, I'll be trying to present them as objectively as possible, while still answering them to the best of my ability.

Finally, we'll talk about how it has worked out for me. I'll be giving you my own, step by step journey of accepting a Stoic mindset. I would love to tell you that it was extremely easy, and all it took was reading two or three texts for me to become a full-blown Stoic. Unfortunately, reality is rarely as kind as to make such drastic changes easy. In fact, I'm still nowhere close to the ideal Stoic. I still sometimes get driven by emotion, sometimes I fall into a rut and it takes me a while to get out of it, sometimes I get nervous. Stoicism hasn't made me perfect, but I'm convinced it has made me better.

The Criticisms of Stoicism

First off, let's tackle an easy criticism:

Stoicism argues that people should repress their emotions. Scientific research has shown that this is detrimental to mental health, hence Stoicism is detrimental to mental health.

See, this criticism stems not from objective reasoning, but rather, from a misunderstanding of Stoicism.

The Stoic doctrine doesn't say that we need to repress our emotions. Rather, it says that we should realize that external factors cannot be bad, and hence there will eventually be no reason for those emotions to arise in the first place. If they're already there, Stoicism teaches us to accept them, and use them as motivation. Both of these things are very different from repressing.

Stoicism also doesn't have any problems with most positive emotions. Since emotions like joy don't lead us into flawed actions, Stoicism has nothing against it. Only emotions like fear or anger, that can actively impede our functioning as reasoning beings, are considered to be given rise from false judgments.

Accepting emotions is the act of understanding why you feel a certain way, and that you do feel that way. This is a level of self-understanding which has been demonstrated to help with mental health issues. Afterwards, your task is to simply accept them, not repress them, but keep them from impeding your function as a human being.

Alternatively, they will be used as motivation. I doubt anyone will say that a student that studies to spite the teacher that dislikes them is doing something unhealthy. While this isn't strictly Stoic (as it is done out of anger.) It is an example of using emotions as motivation, rather than a constraint.

Onto the next one:

Making the statement that eudaimonia can be achieved entirely through pursuit of virtue has uncertain truth value. After all, a sage is not a common person, and it is almost impossible to verify whether someone has achieved eudaimonia. For example, Epicureanism included more factors than virtue in the achievement of eudaimonia.

Now, I'm not going to lie, this criticism has some legs to stand on. Proving that someone has reached eudaimonia is indeed impossible. After all, it is entirely an internal state. Until our MRI machines are advanced enough to be able to recognize even states like that, I'm afraid we won't know if it's truly possible to achieve eudaimonia.

On the other hand, let's look at someone that's most likely, at least according to popular belief, to have achieved it- Buddha. According to Buddhist religion, Buddha became enlightened (reached eudaimonia.) Entirely through the pursuit of virtue and leaving the self behind. The Stoic and Buddhist philosophies are very similar, so if we agree that the Buddha achieved Eudaimonia, then we would agree with Stoicism.

But let's for a second assume that the criticism is true. After all, to a certain degree I would even say it is. It is nigh-impossible to obtain such mental control that things like physical torture or chemical drugs won't affect you. These externals fundamentally alter the biological makeup of the Stoic, and no matter his conviction, are bound to break him away from the enlightened state of eudaimonia.

With that being said, I would say that eudaimonia, being an ancient Greek invention (long before we knew about mind-altering drugs.) Excludes such extreme examples. Theoretically, I can see even physical torture getting conquered (though that would be bordering on mental illness in reality.)

But yes, in the end I do agree that total eudaimonia is practically impossible, but so what? Stoicism isn't about attaining virtue, at its core Stoicism is about the process of obtaining virtue, rather than the final goal of eudaimonia. While that is the final frontier of Stoicism, if you have not reached eudaimonia, you have not failed as a Stoic, for the very pursuit of it is considered virtuous.

The next criticism we'll be looking at strikes at the very building blocks of stoic philosophy:

The way Stoic philosophy refers to nature is extremely vague and hard to justify. Is this "nature" the same nature we think of when we use the word in modern times? If that is the case, then it would be quite difficult to draw moral conclusions from it. Alternatively, is it the divine nature, is it logos? Sure, that works if you're a religious person, but it makes Stoicism rely on theism to exist. Does nature refer to an individual's ideal nature? Sure, that could work, but we aren't exactly certain on what that means.

Personally, I think this is one of the more fun questions to think about, however, I believe the answer can be fairly simple I believe that the issue from which this criticism stems is treating Stoicism as a religion.

Stoicism has no holy book and is an adaptable philosophy. It isn't an issue if the ancient Greeks used one thing for nature and we use a different one. If their idea didn't work, then it is our duty as Stoics to update our philosophy.

As a more clear-cut answer, I would say it is the ideal nature of an individual. Wherein within the ideal nature of a human altruism and reasonableness are found.

Finally, let us look at Nietzche's lengthy criticism of Stoicism presented in his book "Beyond Good And Evil"

"You desire to LIVE "according to Nature"? Oh, you noble Stoics, what fraud of words! Imagine to yourselves a being like Nature, boundlessly extravagant, boundlessly indifferent, without purpose or consideration, without pity or justice, at once fruitful and barren and uncertain: imagine to yourselves INDIFFERENCE as a power--how COULD you live in accordance with such indifference? To live--is not that just endeavoring to be otherwise than this Nature? Is not living valuing, preferring, being unjust, being limited, endeavoring to be different? And granted that your imperative, "living according to Nature," means actually the same as "living according to life"--how could you do

DIFFERENTLY? Why should you make a principle out of what you yourselves are, and must be? In reality, however, it is quite otherwise with you: while you pretend to read with rapture the canon of your law in Nature, you want something quite the contrary, you extraordinary stage-players and self-deluders! In your pride you wish to dictate your morals and ideals to Nature, to Nature herself, and to incorporate them therein; you insist that it shall be Nature "according to the Stoa," and would like everything to be made after your own image, as a vast, eternal glorification and generalism of Stoicism! With all your love for truth, you have forced yourselves so long, so persistently, and with such hypnotic rigidity to see Nature FALSELY, that is to say, Stoically, that you are no longer able to see it otherwise-- and to crown all, some unfathomable superciliousness gives you the Bedlamite hope that BECAUSE you are able to tyrannize over yourselves--Stoicism is self-tyranny--Nature will also allow herself to be tyrannized over: is not the

Stoic a PART of Nature? . . . But this is an old and everlasting story: what happened in old times with the Stoics still happens today, as soon as ever a philosophy begins to believe in itself. It always creates the world in its own image; it cannot do otherwise; philosophy is this tyrannical impulse itself, the most spiritual Will to Power, the will to "creation of the world," the will to the causa prima".

Now then, this is quite a powerful Critique (Nietzsche isn't hailed as one of the greatest philosophers of all time for nothing.) Let's see if we can respond to it step by step:

"You desire to LIVE "according to Nature"? Oh, you noble Stoics, what fraud of words! Imagine to yourselves a being like Nature, boundlessly extravagant, boundlessly indifferent, without purpose or consideration, without pity or justice, at once fruitful and barren and uncertain: imagine to yourselves INDIFFERENCE as a power--how COULD you live in accordance with such indifference? "

This, in my opinion, is the weakest portion of the critique. As we've discussed before, this stems from a misunderstanding of Stoicism and its values. It is not indifference that is a power, but rather acceptance, growth, and antifragility.

"To live--is not that just endeavoring to be otherwise than this Nature? Is not living valuing, preferring, being unjust, being limited, endeavoring to be different? And granted that your imperative, "living according to Nature," means actually the same as "living according to life"--how could you do DIFFERENTLY? Why should you make a principle out of what you yourselves are, and must be? "

This is actually an excellent point, depending on our understanding of nature. Nietzsche suffered here because he had grown up close to our time, when nature had already begun to be understood as, basically "the outside world". In this sense, he is completely right to say that we must live in accordance with nature. On the other hand, if we take nature as the ideal nature we've talked before, then suddenly he has much less of a point. Of course, we can live without virtue, countless people already do.

"In reality, however, it is quite otherwise with you: while you pretend to read with rapture the canon of your law in Nature, you want something quite the contrary, you extraordinary stage-players and self-deluders! In your pride you wish to dictate your morals and ideals to Nature, to Nature herself, and to incorporate them therein; you insist that it shall be Nature "according to the Stoa," and would like everything to be made after your own image, as a vast, eternal glorification and generalism of Stoicism"!

Nietzsche is an excellent writer; however, this passage is essentially naught but rote insults. Stoicism does the precise opposite of this, rather than trying to make nature fit our views, we create all our views to reflect nature.

"With all your love for truth, you have forced yourselves so long, so persistently, and with such hypnotic rigidity to see Nature FALSELY, that is to say, Stoically, that you are no longer able to see it otherwise- and to crown all, some unfathomable superciliousness gives you the Bedlamite hope that BECAUSE you are able to tyrannize over yourselves--Stoicism is self-tyranny--Nature will also allow herself to be tyrannized over: is not the Stoic a PART of Nature?"

Here, I believe, Nietzsche is most understandable in his view. He believes that the Stoic way of thinking is self-tyranny and limiting to the human condition. On the other hand, I fail to see how being able to control one's own emotions is self-tyranny. After all, shouldn't maximizing one's own potential be the goal of all people? Stoicism doesn't repress negativity, rather it serves to steer it and prevent it from ever happening. The "nature will not be tyrannized over" part seems to be just a simple ad-hominem attack, for as much as Nietzsche was a good philosopher, he also loved a good insult.

"But this is an old and everlasting story: what happened in old times with the Stoics still happens today, as soon as ever a philosophy begins to believe in itself. It always creates the world in its own image; it cannot do otherwise; philosophy is this tyrannical impulse itself, the most spiritual Will to Power, the will to "creation of the world," the will to the causa prima".

There isn't much to discuss here, it's mostly a simple verbal attack. On the other hand, it does raise a good question. Is Stoicism only convincing itself reality is in a way which it is not? I would argue that is false, mostly due to the fact that if it were so, Stoicism would need to adapt swiftly, as its whole point is to be in tune with nature.

Personal Problems with Stoicism

It can sometimes be hard to come to terms with living as a Stoic. Even if you truly believe in the Stoic ideology, it isn't the easiest to just jump in and abide by it.

After all, going from being affected by suffering, to accepting, or even using it, is not a process that can be finished in mere days. I wish I could tell you that once you're finished with this book, you'll be able to just go outside and apply all that it has taught you. Unfortunately, that is not the case. You'll struggle, a lot I'd wager. And who wouldn't? Practically our whole lives, we've been taught to live a certain way, and it isn't the Stoic way, I'll tell you that much.

Having problems when you're just starting out living as a Stoic is perfectly normal. Nobody expects you to reach eudaimonia tomorrow (or at all.) As long as you're constantly working towards it, you're doing great!

Try to keep in mind the principles and pillars. After all, they are practically the core of Stoic philosophy. They also let you have an easier time with recognizing what needs to improve. Rather than just realizing you're not quite managing to live as a Stoic, you'll be able to pinpoint your issue, and find a fix for it sooner rather than later.

With that being said, the next chapter includes exercises for you to do once you're ready to make the switch fully.

The most common things to have issues with is accepting and using strong emotions. This is even more difficult than not acting on them. Stopping yourself from acting on impulse is the first step. Unfortunately, acceptance and motivation are things you must master for yourself.

My Experience with Stoicism

Now, given that I'm the author of this book, it would stand to reason I was practically a born Stoic right? I once read a book about it and I instantly not only understood Stoicism, but applied it in my daily life, is how the story should go, right?

Well, I'm sorry to disappoint you, but that's about as far away from the truth as possible. It's true that Stoicism did indeed change my life for the better, however, it did not happen overnight, nor was it as effortless as reading a book. So, let's start from the beginning, shall we?

So, ever since childhood, I was, for the lack of a better word, antisocial. I spent basically all of my time in my room, avoiding other kids, and later on in life, people. It's not that I didn't like being around people, I would simply get nervous and not know how to act. I stumbled across words and would fidget awkwardly.

I was fairly good at school. I mostly got A's without studying much, which was a lifesaver. I was so good at school, in fact, that once I got my first B in high school I almost had a mental breakdown. I completely shut down and refused to as much as go to school. In the end, I barely graduated. I feel ashamed to admit it, but it really shook me down to the core.

In the end, I got a lousy IT chat support job, which was barely enough for me to even survive. This was mostly due to my refusal to go to college because I was paralyzed by the fear that I would fail again. You see, because I didn't attempt many things, those that I attempted and failed really stuck around.

Eventually, I fell into a rut. I was basically doing nothing but working and browsing the internet 24/7. Out of boredom, I started reading books. Over time, my interests got piqued, and I felt a slight twinge of enjoyment from this.

This is when I encountered Stoicism. I still remember how I devoured pretty much every Stoic book put in front of me. Within a few weeks, I had read all of the influential works of the early Stoics, and I wanted to apply the philosophy to my daily life.

So I tried! I went outside, with the mission to strike up a conversation with a random person, after all I couldn't control their reaction, so what was there to be worried about?

In the end, I didn't talk to anyone on that day. Yet again, I felt like a failure, and it wasn't much in the way of acceptance, rather, it simply drove me deeper into the rut I'd dug for myself.

But over time, I slowly started getting better. I used auto-suggestion to convince myself of Stoic principles (this is when you repeat something to yourself so many times you actually start believing in it.)

One day, I was chatting to a group of 4 people in a bar, and I hadn't even noticed. I wasn't fidgeting, I wasn't tripping over words. It felt amazing. Over time, I started getting promotions, from IT guy, to sys admin, to head of the IT department. Now I'm an entrepreneur with my own business, writing books on the side.

In all honesty, I can barely believe my past, shy self and me today are the same person, and yet here we are. For me, the hardest part of becoming a true Stoic was coming to terms with failure. It was something that was practically impossible for me my whole life. So no matter how much I tried, it didn't seem to go anywhere, but I kept trying. As a test of this, I used something I had been terrified for most of my life- asking girls out. I kept trying until I got a "no thank you." And realized I didn't care. By this time I had gotten plenty of "yes"-es, probably because I was already quite a bit more confident.

These days, I no longer ask girls out as a test (my wife would get angry.) But I still try to fail at something every now and then. It helps me remember how it feels to fail, as well as how to accept the feelings that comes with it and make them not phase me.

Now, without further ado, let me help you learn it too.

Chapter 15: Steps To Take To Start Implementing Stoicism In Your Personal And Financial Life

While the key principles of stoicism are few and straightforward, they imply many other ideas. Many of which can be useful in a modern life that isn't strictly Stoic, but simply strives to build a better life for oneself. Here are some steps to start implementing Stoicism in your life.

ACKNOWLEDGE THAT ALL EMOTIONS COME FROM WITHIN AND THAT WE CREATE OUR OWN FEELINGS

You decide if you like something. You decide if you want something. You decide if you don't like something. Those are decisions that are up to you, not up to the person, place, thing, or idea in question. Yet, so often, we react so automatically to things with a simple emotion or desire that we don't even recognize that our response comes from within. We attribute it to that product.

169

Think about how you feel when you see your favorite food on a plate in front of you, or when you see a favorite person that you haven't seen in a while. Those are feelings and emotions inside of you, created by you, but they're such immediate responses that they feel automatic. They feel almost like they're created by the thing you like.

The same thing occurs during every single buying situation. You might deeply want something, but that want is something inside of you, something you created. You created it and it's an entirely internal thing, so you can just as easily stop it if you so choose. This is such a huge key to personal, professional, and financial success. You create your emotional responses, and you can turn them off if you choose to do so. They're all within you.

FIND A RESPECTED MENTOR

When we take emotions out of the equation, our decisions are often reduced down to being based on our understanding of the world, namely the consequences of various options for us and for others.

Over time, experience teaches us quite a lot about these potential consequences of our decisions, but it's never perfect, especially when we're younger.

This is why a mentor is so valuable. A mentor can help us walk through the consequences of various choices that face us in life. A professional mentor can help us make good career decisions, for example. A trusted life mentor – perhaps an older relative that you trust, a pastor, or just someone you respect in the community – can do the same thing for your personal decisions.

Mentors play a powerful role in helping you make decisions outside of the influence of your emotional responses. They usually don't have an emotional stake in your choice, so they can usually look at the options for what they are and help you walk through those options. They can be invaluable, especially when you can tell that emotion is clouding your judgment.

KNOW THAT FAILURE HAPPENS, BUT LIFE GOES ON

One of the most powerful emotions is fear. People are afraid of lots of things: damaging relationships, damaging their career, missing out on something, and so on. The idea of failure seems very negative for most people. The thing is, fear is just another emotion. It's an emotion that tells us that we should never take a risk, that we should avoid failure at all costs.

If we do that, though, we miss out on tons of opportunities. Opportunities in life almost always come with some risk of failure, and that's okay. Failure happens. It's really okay to fail sometimes, as long as you learn something from that failure.

Fear of failure should never hold you back from taking on challenges. Instead, if a challenge or opportunity presents itself, you should evaluate what the actual drawbacks of failure are, how likely they are, and whether you could handle a worst-case scenario. Nothing cuts through fear like looking at the reality of what could happen if things don't go quite right and directly comparing that to the real benefits of taking that risk.

Fear is an emotion, like any other. When you realize that and step away from it, many professional, personal, and financial risks look very different.

READ AND LEARN WITH PURPOSE AND APPLY YOUR NEW KNOWLEDGE

Part of the value of stoicism comes from being able to evaluate people, places, things, situations, and ideas without emotion interfering with that judgment. To do so requires knowledge and the ability to apply that knowledge. Thus, one of the strongest ways to become a better person in terms of properly evaluating the world is to become smarter, to build up your knowledge, and to be able to apply that knowledge in the world.

If you feel uncertain and afraid about financial decisions, for example, the best response isn't to quake in fear and postpone those decisions. The best response is to learn. Go to the library and check out some books on investing and personal finance. Learn more about those issues so they no longer seem scary and unknown. If you do that, it becomes much easier to remove the emotion from those kinds of decisions and to truly make the best decision for you.

BE BRUTALLY HONEST WITH YOURSELF

No one is perfect. We often hold inflated views of ourselves because it feels good to think that we're above average and highly competent. The problem is that an inflated view of oneself can lead them to not bother to improve themselves. And that leads to gradually falling behind others while still maintaining that self-impression of being above average. When that happens, you begin to get passed over in many aspects of life – job promotions, relationships, and so on – and it doesn't make sense to you. That can cause anger, jealousy, and many other negative reactions that mostly serve to cover up the reality of what's happening.

The best solution is to be brutally honest with yourself. How do your skills line up next to your peers? In what areas do their skills exceed yours? In what areas are you more skilled? In what areas can you improve yourself?

This does not extend to "brutal honesty" with others. "Brutal honesty" with others is a cover for being cruel, which has tons of negative social consequences that no one wants in their life.

REFLECT ON YOUR TIME USE

It should be obvious by now that stoicism ties heavily into self-reliance and self-improvement. Stoicism requires you to put emotions aside, see the world for what it is as much as possible, and be brutally honest with yourself about your place in the world and the attributes you have on offer. This almost always results in a strong drive to improve yourself through acquiring knowledge, getting in better shape, and other aspects of self-improvement.

The challenge for many people is finding the time to do this, and quite honestly, time management itself is a great area in which you can improve yourself.

It often directly leads to more time that you can use for improving various aspects of your life. Take a strong, serious look at how you use your time. One great way to do this is to do a time diary. We can use time use trackers like Timing to keep track of how we are using our time. This almost always shows us, in very clear terms, how well we are using our time.

REFLECT ON YOUR MONEY USE

Take a strong, serious look at how you use your money and whether or not it really makes any sense. One great way to do this is to use a spending tracker. Tracking our spending almost always shows us, in very clear terms, how well we are using our money and whether we are wasting it or using it in ways that will continue to bloom in our life.

REFLECT ON YOUR PURPOSE, AND WHETHER YOU'RE ACTUALLY DOING THINGS IN LINE WITH THAT PURPOSE

Thinking about one's purpose in life is a rather deep question, one that often doesn't have an easy answer. It's something I've thought about a lot over the years, and I've come to a small handful of conclusions about what my own purpose in life is – it mostly boils down to helping others and improving myself in all areas. When I do things, I prefer to have them fall into one of those two categories.

Once you've really honed in on a central purpose or two, start looking at the ways in which you spend your time and ask how they're helping you achieve that central purpose in life.

What I've found is that time and time again, when I spend time on things that are more closely related to those two or three central purposes in life, I feel good, and when I do things that aren't related to those central purposes, I feel bad. Thus, using those purposes as a general guide for how to spend my time and how to spend my money makes a lot of sense.

KILL PROCRASTINATION, FOR IT IS YOUR ENEMY

Once you start digging into Stoicism, time management becomes more important to you. The biggest reason is that you don't want to waste time because time wasted is time not spent on the things that are closest to your central purposes in life.

Unsurprisingly, this all points a very negative finger right at procrastination. Procrastination means you're postponing doing something that's important in order to do something that's urgent but perhaps not nearly as important, which is a perfect example of letting emotions run your decision-making process. You want to do something else because the important thing perhaps isn't as fun. The end result is that you end up under-performing on the important task.

The best approach is to start in on important tasks as soon as you learn about them. Start saving for retirement now. Start working on that project now. Even if the initial steps aren't perfect, most of the time they're far better than doing nothing during that time. For a more in depth look, please free to check out my book on Procrastination as well.

Chapter 16: Stoic Quotes

This chapter collects quotes that capture the principles of Stoicism. There are many from the classic Stoics along with some quotes from more modern authors and thinkers. It would be good to remember or jot down a few of these nuggets of wisdoms for stressful times. Of course, practicing these virtues is much more effective than simply memorizing them. May they make your days more meaningful and worry free.

From the Founders

Zeno

No evil is honorable: but death is honorable; therefore death is not evil.

Wellbeing is attained by little and little, and nevertheless is no little thing itself.

Fate is the endless chain of causation, whereby things are; the reason or formula by which the world goes on.

The goal of life is living in agreement with Nature.

If being is many, it must be both like and unlike, and this is impossible, for neither can the like be unlike, nor the unlike like.

We have two ears and one mouth, so we should listen more than we say.

Cleanthes

He has his wish, whose wish can be to have what is enough.

Lead me, Zeus, and you, Fate, wherever you have assigned me. I shall follow without hesitation but even if I am disobedient and do not wish to, I shall follow no less surely.

He needs little who desires but little

Chrysippus

Wise people are in want of nothing, and yet need many things. On the other hand, nothing is needed by fools, for they do not understand how to use anything, but are in want of everything.

The universe itself is God and the universal outpouring of its soul.

Though is the fountain of speech.

If I had followed the multitude, I should not have studied philosophy.

Living virtuously is equal to living in accordance with one's experience of the actual course of nature.

From the Roman Late Stoics

Seneca

All cruelty springs from weakness.

It is a rough road that leads to the heights of greatness.

Most powerful is he who has himself in his own power.

Religion is regarded by the common people as true, by the wise as false, and by the rulers as useful.

Sometimes even to live is an act of courage.

A sword never kills anybody; it is a tool in the killer's hand.

No man was ever wise by chance.

The day which we fear as our last is but the birthday of eternity.

The bravest sight in the world is to see a great man struggling against adversity.

It is quality rather than quantity that matters.

Many men will meet me who are drunkards, lustful, ungrateful, greedy, and excited by the frenzy of ambition. He will view all these as benignly as a physician does his patients.

True happiness is to enjoy the present, without anxious dependence upon the future, not to amuse ourselves with either hopes or fears but to rest satisfied with what we have, which is sufficient, for he that is so wants nothing.

Epictetus

Wealth consists not in having great possessions, but in having few wants.

Only the educated are free.

Men are disturbed not by things, but by the view which they take of them.

If you want to improve, be content to be thought foolish and stupid.

We have two ears and one mouth so that we can listen twice as much as we speak.

There is only one way to happiness and that is to cease worrying about things which are beyond the power of our will.

First say to yourself what you would be; and then do what you have to do.

It's not what happens to you, but how you react to it that matters.

The key is to keep company only with people who uplift you, whose presence calls forth your best.

Remember, it is not enough to be hit or insulted to be harmed, you must believe that you are being harmed. If someone succeeds in provoking you, realize that your mind is complicit in the provocation. Which is why it is essential that we not respond impulsively to impressions; take a moment before reacting, and you will find it easier to maintain control.

No greater thing is created suddenly, any more than a bunch of grapes or a fig. If you tell me that you desire a fig, I answer you that there must be time. Let it first blossom, then bear fruit, then ripen.

Not every difficult and dangerous thing is suitable for training, but only that which is conducive to success in achieving the object of our effort.

Marcus Aurelius

Accept the things to which fate binds you, and love the people with whom fate brings you together, but do so with all your heart.

Everything we hear is an opinion, not a fact. Everything we see is a perspective, not the truth.

Never let the future disturb you. You will meet it, if you have to, with the same weapons of reason which today arm you against the present.

Waste no more time arguing about what a good man should be. Be one.

The object of life is not to be on the side of the majority, but to escape finding one's self in the ranks of the insane.

How much more grievous are the consequences of anger than the causes of it?

It is not death that a man should fear, but he should fear never beginning to live.

When you arise in the morning, think of what a precious privilege it is to be alive—to breathe, to think, to enjoy, to love.

If it is not right do not do it; if it is not true do not say it.

You have power over your mind—not outside events. Realize this, and you will find strength.

Begin the morning by saying to thyself, I shall meet with the busy-body, the ungrateful, arrogant, deceitful, envious, unsocial.

If you are distressed by anything external, the pain is not due to the thing itself, but to your estimate of it; and this you have the power to revoke at any moment.

From Modern Authors

Markus Zusak, The Book Thief

Imagine smiling after a slap in the face. Then think of doing it twenty-four hours a day.

Erin Hunter, Into the Wild

Warriors should suffer their pain silently.

Nora Roberts, Midnight Bayou

Feeling too much is a hell of a lot better than feeling nothing.

Edith Hamilton, The Greek Way

The Greeks not only face facts. They have no desire to escape from them.

Oliver Burkeman, The Antidote: Happiness for People Who Can't Stand Positive Thinking

Confronting the worst-case scenario saps it of much of its anxiety-inducing power. Happiness reached via positive thinking can be fleeting and brittle, negative visualization generates a vastly more dependable calm.

Jane Austen, Sense and Sensibility

Always resignation and acceptance. Always prudence and honor and duty.

Bertrand Russell, A History of Western Philosophy

If virtue is the sole good, there can be no reason against cruelty and injustice, since, as the Stoics are never tired of pointing out, cruelty and injustice afford the sufferer the best opportunities for the exercise of virtue.

Salman Rushdie, Step Across This Line: Collected Nonfiction 1992-2002

How do you defeat terrorism? Don't be terrorized.

Natasha Solomons, Mr. Rosenblum Dreams in English

He liked the English and their peculiarities. He liked their stoicism under pressure; on the wall in his factory he kept a copy of a war poster emblazoned with the Crown of King George and underneath the words "Keep Calm and Carry On."

Jean-Paul Sartre, L'âge de raison (The Age of Reason)

Various well-bred moralities had already discreetly offered him their services: disillusioned epicureanism, smiling tolerance, resignation, common sense stoicism—all the aids whereby a man may savor, minute by minute, like a connoisseur, the failure of a life.

Conclusion

As you learn to live your life as a Stoic, you will right away start to see tremendous benefits start to come your way. You will quickly gain a deeper understanding of the things in life which you value versus those you can (and perhaps should) do without, adopt a natural tendency to focus on your character and improving yourself as an individual through your day to day actions, tap into the immense gratitude which you are capable of applying to all aspects of life, and find a sense of unshakeable calm no matter what each day brings.

Yes, by being a Stoic, you tend to know yourself better than before. You will know the specific things that you like, the things that you dislike, and the things that truly have value for you. Hence, it becomes easier for you to improve your personality and character, thus, making you a better person. Also, you become less likely to feel overwhelmed in the very distressing situations of your life. As a Stoic, you understand that you won't live forever, and that you need to cherish and make the best out of your everyday life.

No matter how challenging life's adversities may seem, the practices of Stoicism will empower you to flip life's script and look on the bright side in all things. With practice and perseverance, you will begin to see the good in all situations, even the seemingly negative ones, without even trying. With this newly honed sense of perspective, you can now effortlessly transform life's obstacles into opportunities for growth. Situations that used to cause you distress will no longer overwhelm you, but instead, make you a stronger person emotionally and improve your character.

As you proceed through life with this new base of Stoic knowledge at hand, bear in mind that you must always keep a keen eye on your sense of entitlement. This is a theme that lies at the core of so many Stoic beliefs and ways of viewing life's situations. When you recognize the role that entitlement plays in your negative emotions, you can release it and proceed to make decisions and choices in life without bias and with a clear head. By relinquishing your sense of entitlement, you create space for sound judgment in all of life's trials.

CPSIA information can be obtained
at www.ICGtesting.com
Printed in the USA
BVHW061008210321
603119BV00004B/681